Editorial Project Manager
Eric Migliaccio

Editor in Chief
Karen J. Goldfluss, M.S. Ed.

Cover Artist
Sarah Kim

Illustrator
Clint McKnight

Art Coordinator
Renée Mc Elwee

Imaging
James Edward Grace

Publisher
Mary D. Smith, M.S. Ed.

Author

Ruth Foster, M.Ed.

For the Lexile measures of the reading passages included in this book, visit *www.teachercreated.com* and click on the Lexile Measures button located on this resource's product page.

For correlations to the Common Core State Standards, see pages 95–96 of this book or visit *http://www.teachercreated.com/standards*.

Teacher Created Resources, Inc.
12621 Western Avenue
Garden Grove, CA 92841
www.teachercreated.com
ISBN: 978-1-4206-2692-6

© 2017 Teacher Created Resources, Inc.
Made in U.S.A.

Table of Contents

Overview

What Is Close Reading?

Close reading is thoughtful, critical analysis of a text. Close-reading instruction gives your students guided practice in approaching, understanding, and, ultimately, mastering complex texts. This type of instruction builds positive reading habits and allows students to successfully integrate their prior experiences and background knowledge with the unfamiliar text they are encountering.

There are certain factors that differentiate close-reading instruction from other types of reading instruction. These factors include the types of **texts** used for instruction, the **tasks** students are asked to perform, and the **questions** they are expected to answer. For detailed information on these factors, see "A Closer Look" on pages 4–5.

What Are Text-Dependent Questions?

Text-dependent questions (TDQs) can only be answered by referring explicitly back to the text. They are designed to deepen the reader's understanding of the text, and they require students to answer in such a way that higher-level thinking is demonstrated. To be most effective, TDQs should address all that a reading passage has to offer; the questions asked should prompt students to consider the meaning, purpose, structure, and craft contained within the text.

How Is This Guide Organized?

The units in *Close Reading with Text-Dependent Questions* are divided into two sections. Each of the twenty **Section I Units** (pages 8–87) is a four-page unit.

Page 1 **Close-Reading Passage**	This page contains a short, complex, high-interest reading passage. Parts of the passage are numbered for easy reference, and space for annotation is provided in the left margin and between lines of text.
Page 2 **Close-Reading Tasks**	Students are guided to read the passage, summarize it, reread and annotate it, and meet with a partner to discuss and define the author's word choices.
Page 3 **Text-Dependent Questions**	Students are asked to display a general understanding of the text, locate key details within it, cite evidence, and begin to use tools such as inference.
Page 4 **More TDQs**	Students examine the structure of the text and the author's purpose. They form opinions and use evidence to support and defend claims. A research prompt encourages choice, exploration, and cross-curricular connections. (**Note:** Monitor students' Internet research for content appropriateness.)

Each of the two **Section II Units** (pages 88–91) contains two pages.

Page 1 **Close-Reading Passage**	This page contains a short, complex, high-interest reading passage. Parts of the passage are numbered for easy reference, and space for annotation is provided in the left margin and between lines of text.
Page 2 **Peer-Led Tasks**	This page guides groups of students through a series of peer-led tasks in which each member is assigned a different role. Students become teachers to one another as they work together to analyze a text.

A Closer Look

Close Reading with Text-Dependent Questions focuses on the three main components of close-reading instruction: the **texts** students are asked to read, the **tasks** they are instructed to perform, and the **text-dependent questions (TDQs)** they are expected to answer thoughtfully and accurately.

The Texts

- ✓ short
- ✓ complex
- ✓ high-interest
- ✓ multi-genre

Not all texts are appropriate for close-reading instruction. Passages need to be written in a manner that invites analysis and at a level that requires slow, careful, deliberate reading. The texts in this guide achieve these goals in a number of ways.

- **Length:** Close-reading passages should be relatively short because the rigorous work required of students could make longer passages overwhelming.

Each unit in this guide contains a one-page passage of about 325–350 words. This is an ideal length to introduce and explore a subject, while allowing students of this age to conduct an in-depth examination of its content and purpose.

- **Complexity:** The best way to foster close reading of informational or fictional text is through text complexity. Writing achieves a high level of text complexity when it fulfills certain factors. The **purpose** of the text is implicit or hidden in some way, and the **structure** of the text is complex and/or unconventional. The **demands** of the text ask students to use life experiences, cultural awareness, and content knowledge to supplement their understanding. The **language** of the text incorporates domain-specific, figurative, ironic, ambiguous, or otherwise unfamiliar vocabulary.

The passages in this guide contain all of these different types of language and ask students to decipher their meanings in the context of the parts (words, phrases, sentences, etc.) around them. The passages meet the purpose and structure criteria by delaying key information, defying reader expectations, and/or including unexpected outcomes — elements that challenge students to follow the development of ideas along the course of the text. Students must combine their prior knowledge with the information given in order to form and support an opinion.

- **Interest:** Since close reading requires multiple readings, it is vital that the topics covered and style employed be interesting and varied. The passages in this resource will guide your students down such high-interest avenues as adventure, invention, discovery, and oddity. These texts are written with humor and wonder, and they strive to impart the thrill of learning.

- **Text Types and Genres:** It is important to give students experience with the close reading of a wide variety of texts. The passages in this guide are an equal mix of fiction and nonfiction; and they include examples and/or combinations of the following forms, text types, and genres: drama, poetry, descriptive, narrative, expository, and argumentative.

- **Lexile-Leveled:** A Lexile measure is a quantitative tool designed to represent the complexity of a text. The passages featured in this resource have been Lexile-leveled to ensure their appropriateness for this grade level. For more information, visit this resource's product page at *www.teachercreated.com.*

A Closer Look (cont.)

The Tasks

✓ read and reread
✓ summarize
✓ annotate
✓ collaborate
✓ connect
✓ illustrate
✓ cite and support
✓ ask and answer

An essential way in which close-reading instruction differs from other practices can be seen in the tasks students are asked to perform. This resource focuses on the following student tasks:

- **Read and Reread:** First and foremost, close reading requires multiple readings of the text. This fosters a deeper understanding as the knowledge gained with each successive reading builds upon the previous readings. To keep students engaged, the tasks associated with each reading should vary. When students are asked to reread a passage, they should be given a new purpose or a new group of questions that influences that reading.

- **Annotation:** During at least one reading of the passage, students should annotate, or make notes on, the text. Annotation focuses students' attention on the text and allows them to track their thought processes as they read. It also allows students to interact with the text by noting words, phrases, or ideas that confuse or interest them. When writing about or discussing a text, students can consult their annotations and retrieve valuable information.

For more information about annotation, see pages 6–7 of this guide.

- **Additional Tasks:** Collaboration allows students to discuss and problem-solve with their partner peers. An emphasis is placed on demonstrating an understanding of unfamiliar words in context and applying academic vocabulary in new ways. Throughout, students are prompted to cite evidence to support claims and reinforce arguments. Often, students are asked to illustrate written information or connect text to visuals. A section of peer-led activities (pages 88–91) encourages students to ask and answer peer-generated questions.

The TDQs

✓ general
✓ key details
✓ word choice
✓ sequence
✓ structure
✓ purpose
✓ inference
✓ opinion

Text-dependent questions (TDQs) emphasize what the text has to offer as opposed to the students' personal experiences. This helps students focus on the text — from the literal (what it says) to the structural (how it works) to the inferential (what it means).

The TDQs in this resource ask students to demonstrate a wide range of understanding about the text. There is a progression from questions that ask for general understanding to those that require deeper levels of focus. The first question or two are relatively easy to answer, as this promotes student confidence and lessens the possibility for discouragement or disengagement. Subsequent questions delve into increasingly higher-order involvement in the text. Students are asked why a passage is written the way it is and if they feel that the author's choices were ultimately successful. This type of instruction and questioning not only makes students better readers, it also makes them better writers as they consider the decisions authors make and the effects those choices have on the text and the reader.

All About Annotation
Teacher Instructions

Annotation is the practice of making notes on a text during reading, and it is a crucial component of the close-reading process. It allows students to more deeply dissect a text and make note of the parts that intrigue or excite them, as well as the parts that confuse or disengage them. Annotation gives students a tool with which to interact with the text on their terms and in ways specific to their needs and interests.

Tips and Strategies

☑ This resource has been designed to give your students the space needed to annotate the reading passages. Extra space has been included in the margin to the left of the passage. In addition, room has also been added between each line of text, with even more space included between paragraphs.

☑ Share the student sample (page 7) to give your students an idea of what is expected of them and how annotation works. This sample only shows three basic ways of annotating: circling unfamiliar words, underlining main ideas, and writing key details. Begin with these to ensure that students understand the concept. Additional responsibilities and tasks can be added later.

☑ Much like the skill of summarization requires restraint, so does annotation. Give students a goal. For example, tell them they can only underline one main idea per paragraph and/or their key notes for each paragraph can be no more than five words in length. If these expectations aren't given, students might make too many notes, circle too many words, and underline too much text. This would make the text more difficult to read and create the opposite effect of what is intended.

☑ If you see that a majority of your students are circling the same unfamiliar words and noting confusion in the same areas of the text, spend more time and focus on these parts.

☑ Instruct students to reference their annotations when answering more complex questions, such as those inquiring about the structural and inferential elements of the text.

☑ Annotations can be used as an assessment tool to determine how well students are analyzing a text or even how well they are following directions.

☑ If students need more room to annotate, consider allowing them to affix sticky notes onto their pages and add notes in this way.

☑ As students become more fluent at the skill of annotating, increase their responsibilities and/or add new tasks. Here are a few examples to consider:

♦ Add a question mark (?) for information they find confusing.

♦ Add an exclamation point (!) for information they find surprising.

♦ Draw arrows between ideas and/or elements to show connections.

♦ Keep track of characters' names and relationships.

♦ Add notes about such elements of authorial craft as tone, mood, or style.

All About Annotation *(cont.)*
Student Sample

Annotation = making notes on a text as you read it

3 Basic Ways to Annotate a Text

Note key details.	**Circle difficult words.**	**Underline main ideas.**
In the left margin, write a few words that give key details from the paragraph. Your notes in this space should be brief. They should be five words or fewer.	If you aren't sure what a word means, circle it. Once you determine its meaning, write the word's definition in the left margin and circle it.	Find the main idea of each paragraph and underline it. The main idea gives the most important information the author is trying to tell you in that paragraph.

Wriggling for Bones

asked son
dark cave
danger

1   Dr. Lee Berger asked his son Matt to do a task. The (task) was not easy. First, Matt had to go into a dark cave. Inside the cave, Matt had to climb up a big pile of rocks. The pile was so big it had a name. It was called the Dragon's Back, and it was extremely steep and jagged. <u>Matt had to be very careful.</u> If he slipped and fell, he could cut himself on the sharp, rough points of the rocks.

very tight
space

2   After Matt climbed Dragon's Back, he had to (wriggle) through a small opening. Once Matt wriggled through this opening, he had to go down a crack. <u>The crack was very narrow.</u> It was only about seven and one-half inches wide! Matt had to squeeze down this narrow crack for more than 30 feet!

Wriggling for Bones

 Dr. Lee Berger asked his son Matt to do a task. The task was not easy. First, Matt had to go into a dark cave. Inside the cave, Matt had to climb up a big pile of rocks. The pile was so big it had a name. It was called the Dragon's Back, and it was extremely steep and jagged. Matt had to be very careful. If he slipped and fell, he could cut himself on the sharp, rough points of the rocks.

 After Matt climbed Dragon's Back, he had to wriggle through a small opening. Once Matt wriggled through this opening, he had to go down a crack. The crack was very narrow. It was only about seven and one-half inches wide! Matt had to squeeze down this narrow crack for more than 30 feet!

 There was a chamber at the end of the crack. The chamber was filled with bones. Matt's father wanted Matt to look all around the little room. He wanted him to look closely at the bones. When Matt came out, his father forgot to ask Matt if he was okay. He forgot to ask Matt if he had been scared. Matt's father just asked, "And?" All Matt said was, "Daddy, it's wonderful!"

 Dr. Berger knew that spelunkers often find old things in caves. For that reason, Dr. Berger asked any cave explorer who saw bones to bring him photos. When Dr. Berger first saw the photos of the bones in the cave, he thought they might be something special. Wanting to be sure, Dr. Berger asked his son Matt to take a closer look.

 Dr. Berger then found six very skinny people to get the bones out of the little room. The bones were special. They were very old. Dr. Berger learned a lot about the past from the bones. He could tell that the bones had been carefully put in the chamber. Dr. Berger was very lucky that the spelunkers had found them!

Your Name: _____   Partner: _____

Wriggling for Bones (cont.)

First   Silently read "Wriggling for Bones." You might see words you do not know. There might be parts you do not understand. Keep reading! Try to find out what the story is mainly about.

Then   Sum up the story. Write the main actions and most important information. If someone reads your summary, that person should know it is this story you are writing about.

_____

_____

_____

_____

_____

After That   Read the story again. Use a pencil to circle or mark words you don't know. Note places that confuse you. Underline the main action or idea of each paragraph.

Next   Meet with your partner. Help each other find these words in the text.

task   jagged   narrow   chamber   spelunker

Read the sentences around the words. Think about how they fit in the story. Which key words or phrases from the text help you define them? Complete the chart.

Word	Meaning	Key Words or Phrases
task	a job or chore, something you have to do	Matt had to go into a dark cave and climb up a pile of sharp rocks.
jagged		
narrow		
chamber		
spelunker		

Your Name: _____

Wriggling for Bones *(cont.)*

Now   Answer the story questions below.

1. How did Dr. Berger know there were bones in the cave? _____

_____

2. Why do you think Dr. Berger didn't go into the chamber and get the bones himself? Use these words from the story as part of your answer: seven and one-half inches wide.

_____

_____

_____

3. Do you think Matt liked the task his father gave him? Use evidence from the story to support your answer.

_____

_____

_____

_____

4. Think about the pile of rocks that was called Dragon's Back. Draw a picture of what you think a dragon's back might look like.

Why do you think that name was chosen? Use some of the descriptive words from the first paragraph in your answer. For example, you might use the word *steep*.

_____

_____

_____

_____

_____

_____

_____

Your Name: _____

Wriggling for Bones *(cont.)*

Then Reread the entire story one last time. Pay attention to how the first three paragraphs differ from the last two.

5. The first three paragraphs focus mainly on _____

_____

while the last two paragraphs are mostly about _____

_____

6. What do you think is the author's purpose for beginning the story in this way? Explain.

_____

_____

_____

_____

7. The author could have started the story a different way. She could have said: *Draw a line seven and a half inches long.* Write a sentence that could follow this new first line.

Draw a line seven and a half inches long. _____

_____

_____

Do you think this new beginning would change the story? Do you think it would make it better or worse? Explain. (There is no wrong answer! It is what you think.)

_____

_____

_____

_____

Learn More Use the Internet to look up Rising Star Cave in South Africa. Locate pictures of people in the cave and of the bones. Find one new piece of information that you think would have fit well into the "Wriggling for Bones" passage. On the back of this paper, write a short paragraph about this new information.

Key Search Terms
◆ Rising Star Cave
◆ Dr. Berger
◆ bones
◆ underground astronauts

The Ugliest Creature

 Marcella gasped in horror. "What a disgusting creature!" she thought. "I've never seen anything so ugly. Its head is too big for its body. Its warty brown skin is hideous!" The creature Marcella was looking at was a monkfish. It had a huge head and a mouth filled with monstrous razor-sharp teeth. For many years, people didn't want to eat monkfish. They thought its taste matched its appearance. They thought it wouldn't taste good.

 Marcella shuddered when she saw what was in the next exhibit. "This animal is hideous, too," Marcella thought. "It's even more repulsive than the monkfish! What on earth is coming out of its nose?" Marcella was looking at a star-nosed mole. Star-nosed moles have 22 appendages that ring its snout. The appendages are long and fleshy. They look like thick, pink noodles. The appendages are like very sensitive fingers. Without them, the mole would not be able to find its way around or find its prey.

 "This one is the most repulsive of all!" Marcella thought. "What a foul and horrid creature. It's nothing more than a blob!" The creature's name matched its appearance, for the sign in front of the exhibit said it was a blobfish. Blobfish live at the bottom of the ocean. Their flesh is like a mass of Jell-O®. They float above the sea floor and eat what passes by them.

 Marcella looked down at her arms. Looking at all the ugly creatures had made Marcella feel extremely uncomfortable and unsettled. Due to her feelings, Marcella's arms were now covered in bright blue and black rings. "No one has better looking arms than I have," she thought, "especially when I'm feeling unsettled. Not a creature in this world would call them hideous, revolting, or repulsive. They must be the envy of the animal world."

 As Marcella moved through the water, she thought, "Eight is the perfect number of arms to have. And if one gets bitten off, it just grows back! Oh, I'm so fortunite to be a beautiful blue-ringed octopus!"

Your Name: _____   Partner: _____

The Ugliest Creature *(cont.)*

First — Silently read "The Ugliest Creature." You might see words you do not know and read parts you do not understand. Keep reading! Try to find out what the story is mainly about.

Then — Sum up the story. Write the main actions and most important information. If someone reads your summary, that person should know it is this story you are writing about.

_____

_____

_____

_____

_____

After That — Read the story again. Use a pencil to circle or mark words you don't know. Note places that confuse you. Underline the main action or idea of each paragraph.

Next — Meet with your partner. Find all the words in the story that Marcella uses to describe how things look. Together, decide which words are positive and which words are negative.

Positive Words	Negative Words

Choose one word from each list. Explain how the story helped you decide if the word was positive or negative.

	Chosen Word	How the Story Helps
positive		
negative		

Your Name: _____

The Ugliest Creature *(cont.)*

Now Answer the story questions below.

1. What happens if Marcella loses one of her arms? _____

_____

2. Why didn't people want to eat monkfish? _____

_____

What is it about the monkfish that people might find ugly? Use at least one phrase from the story in your answer.

_____

_____

_____

3. In the box, draw a very rough sketch of what you think a star-nosed mole's nose might look like. On the lines, quote some phrases from the passage that helped you know what to draw.

_____

_____

_____

_____

_____

You are told that, "the appendages are like very sensitive fingers." How does this comparison help you understand how the mole finds its way around?

_____

_____

4. What does the author say the blobfish's flesh is like? _____

Would it have been harder to make a mental picture of the blobfish if you didn't know what Jell-O® is? Explain why.

_____

_____

Your Name: _____

The Ugliest Creature *(cont.)*

Then Reread the entire story one last time.

5. Describe when and how you learn exactly what Marcella is.

_____

_____

_____

_____

6. Why do you think the author made the reader wait to find out more about Marcella?

_____

_____

_____

_____

7. A story can use **foreshadowing** to hint at what is to come. The author provides foreshadowing in paragraph 4. How did the author give clues about what you were going to find out about Marcella?

_____

_____

_____

_____

_____

Learn More Find pictures of the monkfish, star-nosed mole, blobfish, and blue-ringed octopus. Take a class vote. Which animal has the most interesting or unique appearance? Mark your votes on a tally chart.

monkfish	ЦHT
mole	ЦHT
blobfish	ЦHT II
octopus	III

Another Idea!

How do you think one of these animals would feel about Marcella? Write a paragraph or two from the point of view of a monkfish, blobfish, or star-nosed mole.

Missing!

 The police were called. Rescue teams came out. Volunteers searched for hours. The police, the rescue teams, and all the volunteers combed the barren, treeless hillsides. Everyone wanted to find the missing woman. They knew that she was five feet and two inches tall. They were told she was wearing dark clothing.

 Iceland is a small island where few people live. In the summer, the sun never sets. In the winter, the sun never rises above the horizon. There are lots of volcanoes, and sometimes these volcanoes erupt. Hot lava streams out, and ash is spewed into the air. People have to flee from their homes. Roads become impassable, and planes must be grounded because the ash might clog up their engines. Iceland has lots of glaciers, too. The glaciers are like huge rivers of ice. The country also has steep cliffs, roaring rivers, and thundering waterfalls. Many people enjoy Iceland's hot springs. People can sit in the hot water while all around them there is snow and ice!

 The missing woman was a tourist in Iceland. Her bus had stopped in a remote volcanic area. Although the spot was out of the way, it was a good place for walking. The bus driver waited for everyone to return to the bus. When one tourist was an hour late, he called the police.

 All of the tourists on the bus wanted to help. They helped search for the missing person. Then one of the tourists found out whom everyone was searching for. They were searching for her! The tourist had been searching for herself for hours!

 The bus driver had not counted the number of passengers correctly. Like the other tourists, the "missing" woman had gone walking. Before she got on the bus, she did something. She changed her clothes! When she got on the bus in her new clothes, no one recognized her. They thought she was someone else.

Your Name: _____   Partner: _____

Missing! *(cont.)*

First) Silently read "Missing!" You might see words you do not know. There might be parts you do not understand. Keep reading! Try to find out what the story is mainly about.

Then) Sum up the story. Write the main actions and most important information. If someone reads your summary, that person should know it is this story you are writing about.

_____

_____

_____

_____

_____

After That) Read the story again. Use a pencil to circle or mark words you don't know. Note places that confuse you. Underline the main action or idea of each paragraph.

Next) Meet with your partner. Working together, pick which hill is barren. Circle it.

Which part or words in "Missing!" helped you pick the barren hill? _____

_____

With your partner, find and quote the part that tells why people must flee their homes.

_____

_____

Most likely, if one **flees**, one is _____.

What is one thing that would make each of you flee?

  ◆ you? _____

  ◆ your partner? _____

Your Name: _____

Missing! *(cont.)*

Now   Answer the story questions below.

1. Why did the bus driver think that the woman was missing? _____

_____

What could the bus driver do in the future to stop this mistake from happening again?

_____

2. In the first paragraph, you are told that everyone **combed** the hillsides. In the space to the right, draw a tiny picture of a comb.

    a. You drew a picture of a thing. In the story, is the word **combed** used as a noun or a verb? Why? (**Remember:** A **noun** is a person, place, or thing. A **verb** tells an action.)

    _____

    _____

    b. When people combed the hillsides, do you think they were using real combs? Explain.

    _____

    _____

3. When people combed the hillsides, do you think they were being careful where they looked or just guessing where the woman might be? Why does the word **combed** make you think this? Why do you think the author used this word?

_____

_____

_____

4. Does Iceland have big rivers? Does it have big waterfalls? Find words in the text that help you answer **yes** or **no**. Explain how the words helped you decide. (**Hint:** The words that help you decide will be two adjectives. Adjectives describe nouns.)

_____

_____

_____

Your Name: _____

Missing! (cont.)

Now Reread the entire story one last time. ———— (Circle one.) ————

5. Which paragraph is the most different from all the others?   1   2   3   4   5

What is this paragraph about? _____

How is it different from the other paragraphs? _____

_____

_____

Why did the author put this paragraph where she put it? Why do you think she did not start the passage with this paragraph?

_____

_____

6. What if you were asked to create an illustration (drawing) to go with this passage? Your illustration should help the reader better understand the information in the story.

Describe what you would draw. _____

_____

_____

How would your drawing be helpful? _____

_____

7. How do you think the woman in the story felt when she found out everyone was looking for her? Explain your answer. Provide some evidence from the passage that hints at how the woman might have felt.

_____

_____

_____

 Learn More Look up Iceland facts. Make a chart in which you compare and contrast facts about Iceland to facts about your state or country. Compare such facts as population, size, climate, landforms, and official language.

The Sky Is Falling!

1 Chicken Small ran to his friend Turkey Burger. "Turkey Burger," Chicken Small said, "We've got a big problem. The sky is falling. I'm not sure what to do."

2 Turkey Burger said, "We've got a serious problem on our hands if the sky is really falling. There's nothing funny about this at all. Indeed, this is not a humorous situation. I'm worried because I don't have a solution for you. Maybe Moose Goose will have an answer for you. I'll come with you, and we can ask together."

3 Chicken Small and Turkey Burger went to Moose Goose. When they told him that they needed a solution to their problem, Moose Goose said, "Oh dear, this is not good. What dismal news! This situation is quite dire. We need to get it fixed right away. Perhaps Skunkie Punkie can help us."

4 Skunkie Punkie sniffed sorrowfully. "Oh dear," she said. "This is terrible news. Your dismal news is making me feel very sad, indeed. We must stop the sky from falling. We must! Perhaps Pearl Squirrel will have an idea."

5 Everyone went in search of Pearl Squirrel. They were all anxious to tell him that the sky was falling. When they finally found him, everyone shouted, "We have dismal news! The situation is dire! The sky is falling!"

6 Pearl Squirrel looked at Chicken Small and Turkey Burger. Pearl Squirrel looked at Moose Goose and Skunkie Punkie. Pearl Squirrel's eyes twinkled, and his mouth began to curl up at the corners. "Chicken Small and Turkey Burger, the situation is not dire at all. It's not such dismal news at all. Moose Goose and Skunkie Punkie, there is nothing to be sorry about."

7 "In fact," Pearl Squirrel said, "I find it quite humorous that you are all so upset. All we have to do is paint another sky. This time we won't use tape to hang it up. We'll staple it onto the back of the stage instead. The show must go on!"

Your Name: _____ Partner: _____

The Sky Is Falling! *(cont.)*

First — Silently read "The Sky Is Falling!" You might see words you do not know. There might be parts you do not understand. Keep reading! Try to find out what the story is mainly about.

Then — Sum up <u>only the first five paragraphs</u>. Write the main actions and most important information. If someone reads your summary, that person should know it is this story you are writing about, not a different story!

_____

_____

_____

_____

_____

_____

After That — Read the story again. Use a pencil to circle or mark words you don't know. Note places that confuse you. Underline the main action or idea of each paragraph.

Next — Meet with your partner. Find the words *humorous* and *dismal* in the story. Discuss how the author helped you understand what each word meant.

	humorous	dismal
Definition: Here is what we think this word means.		
Evidence: Here is why we think it has this meaning.		

Your Name: _____

The Sky Is Falling! *(cont.)*

Now   Answer the story questions below.

1. How did Skunkie Punkie know the sky was falling? _____

_____

2. Did any of the animals ignore or hide from the problem?   ❑ YES   ❑ NO

Defend your answer. Tell why you answered **yes** or **no**. _____

_____

3. In the story, it says that the sky was falling. Explain how this can be both true *and* false.

How it can be true: _____

_____

How it can be false: _____

_____

4. Think about the names of the characters in the story. What do these names tell you about the story? What do you think was the author's purpose for choosing names like these?

_____

_____

_____

Imagine if the story had included illustrations (drawings). Look at the two character drawings below. Which one would better fit the story, **Drawing A** or **Drawing B**? Fill in the bubble beside your answer.

Ⓐ

Ⓑ

Why did you choose this drawing? Explain why it would fit the story better.

_____

_____

_____

_____

_____

_____

Your Name: _____

The Sky Is Falling! *(cont.)*

Then   Read the passage one last time. Think about how it ends.

5. Sum up only the last two paragraphs. Tell what you find out about the sky and how Pearl Squirrel differs from the other animals.

_____

_____

_____

_____

6. What does the author say about Pearl Squirrel's eyes and mouth? Use a quotation to show your answer.

_____

_____

How did this description help you know how Pearl Squirrel felt?

_____

_____

7. Which paragraph tells *which* sky is falling? (Circle one.)   1   2   3   4   5   6   7

How do you think the story would have been different if you found out in the first paragraph that the sky was painted and used to decorate a stage?

_____

_____

In your opinion, would this change have made the story better or worse? Explain.

_____

_____

Learn More   There are many versions of the story "Chicken Little." Find a copy of "Chicken Little" in your library or online. Compare the two. Which do you like better? Can you or your class make up your own version?

Stay Away from My Toys!

 We are always told it is a good thing to share. If one is honest, one knows that sometimes it is very hard to share. When other people play with your toys, they may break them. They may leave them in the dirt or out in the rain. They may carelessly lose pieces of your games. They may mix pieces of several puzzles all together. They might even let their dog bite the head off of your doll! They might tie one of your toys to a string and let the cat pounce on it!

 Robert Louis Stevenson is a famous writer. He was born in 1850 in Scotland. When he was little, he had trouble fitting in. He missed a lot of school due to illness, and other children thought he looked strange. When he was older, he traveled all around the world.

 Stevenson wrote many books. One of his most famous books for children was *Treasure Island*. Packed with adventure, the book has a one-legged seaman with a parrot on his shoulder. It also has pirates and a treasure map marked with an X. Stevenson also wrote poetry. A *Child's Garden of Verses* is a collection of poems he wrote for children. One of the poems in this collection is called "Looking Forward." It goes like this:

> When I am grown to man's estate
>
> I shall be very proud and great,
>
> And tell the other girls and boys
>
> Not to meddle with my toys.

 Stevenson wrote this when he was a grown man, but it shows that he remembers what it was like to be a child. Someone must have told him he had to share his toys, and he didn't like it! Perhaps this is why he was a successful children's author. He remembered what it was like to be a child. He recalled how difficult it was to share. He remembered that he wanted to be able to tell adults who made him share, "No, I won't!"

Your Name: _____ Partner: _____

Stay Away from My Toys! *(cont.)*

First Silently read "Stay Away from My Toys!" You might see words you do not know. There might be parts you do not understand. Keep reading! Try to find out what the story is mainly about.

Then Sum up <u>paragraphs 2–4 only</u>. Do **not** include paragraph 1 in your summary! Write the main actions and most important information. If someone reads your summary, that person should know it is this story you are writing about, not a different story!

_____

_____

_____

_____

_____

After That Read the story again. Use a pencil to circle or mark words you don't know. Note places that confuse you. Underline the main action or idea of each paragraph.

Next Meet with your partner. Find the word *meddle* in the poem "Looking Forward." Together, discuss the meaning of the word *meddle*. Base your discussion on how the word is used in the poem. Then complete the following sentences.

a. After reading part of "Looking Forward," I think the word *meddle* means

_____.

I think this because _____

_____

_____

b. With your partner, share a time when someone meddled with something of yours. Your partner will also share a story with you. Write a quick summary of your partner's story. In your summary, answer these questions: Who meddled? What did that person do? When did this happen? In your summary, use the word *meddle* at least once.

_____

_____

_____

_____

Your Name: _____

Stay Away from My Toys! (cont.)

Now — Answer the story questions below.

1. Write two facts about Robert Louis Stevenson's childhood. State the paragraph(s) in which you found each fact.

Fact About His Choldhood	Paragraph #

2. Why does the author seem to think that the book *Treasure Island* is packed with adventure? Quote some words from the story to defend your answer.

_____

_____

3. The author says that someone might tie a string to one of your toys and then let a cat pounce on it. What do you picture in your mind when you think of a cat pouncing?

_____

_____

_____

Would the picture in your mind be the same if the author just said someone could play with your toy? How would it be different?

_____

_____

_____

4. The poem mentioned in the passage is called "Looking Forward." What stage of life is Robert Louis Stevenson looking forward to? (**Hint:** See the box to the right for stages of life.) Explain how you know this information.

_____

_____

_____

Stages of Life

infancy
early childhood
middle childhood
late childhood
adolescence (teens)
young adulthood
adulthood

Your Name: _____

Stay Away from My Toys! *(cont.)*

Then) Reread the entire story one last time. Think about how paragraph 1 relates to the rest of the passage.

5. Write a very short summary of paragraph 1.

_____

_____

6. Did paragraph 1 give you any hint that the following paragraphs would be about Robert Louis Stevenson? Tell why or why not.

_____

_____

Did paragraph 1 help prepare you for the poem and the last paragraph? Tell why or why not.

_____

_____

_____

7. Reread the poem "Looking Forward." Write down the rhyming words.

_____

_____

Do you think a small child would find the poem easier to listen to because it rhymes? Explain.

_____

_____

Make up a two-line rhyme of your own. It can be about anything.

_____

_____

Learn More) Find out more about Robert Louis Stevenson. See if you can find a copy of his poem titled "My Shadow." Also, see if you can find out why he gave his birthday away and who he gave it to!

Purr for the Perfect Pet

 Brian yearned for a pet so badly that his heart ached. He begged for a dog, but his father said no. His father told him that dogs barked too much. "The small ones never stop yapping or yipping, and the big ones howl at the moon," he said. "There's not going to be a dog in this house, ever," he said, shaking his head.

 His father suggested a fish, but Brian wanted a pet he could pet. A fish wouldn't have soft fur, and it certainly couldn't sit on his lap. Brian suggested a hamster, but his father was adamant that he would not permit it. Speaking firmly, his father said, "No hamsters in this house. I detest rodents. Rodents of any kind are disgusting. I really dislike them. Hamsters are better than mice, but no kind of rodent will ever live in this house."

 Thinking that his father might not detest birds, Brian suggested a canary. "I like the way canaries chirp," his father said, "but the answer is 'no'." When Brian protested, his father remained adamant about his decision. "I don't think it's fair to the bird," his father said. "Birds should not be kept in cages. They should be allowed to soar through the air."

 Brian showed his father a notice he found.

> **FREE cat.**
> **Purrs but doesn't roar.**
> **Chirps like a canary.**

Brian's father read the notice very carefully. "Sounds like a perfect pet," he said, "and I like that it is free. Call and see if anyone has taken it yet. If it's still available, you can go get it right now."

 The cat was still available, so Brian left immediately and brought it home. When Brian's father saw the cat, he was dumbfounded. The cat didn't bark or roar. It purred and chirped like a canary. Still, Brian's father couldn't speak. Perhaps it was because the cat was a cheetah!

Your Name: _____ Partner: _____

Purr for the Perfect Pet (cont.)

First | Silently read "Purr for the Perfect Pet." You might see words you do not know. There might be parts you do not understand. Keep reading! Find out what the story is mainly about.

Then | Sum up the <u>first four paragraphs of the story only</u>. (Do not write about the last paragraph.) Write down the main actions and most important information.

_____

_____

_____

_____

_____

After That | Read the story again. Use a pencil to circle or mark words you don't know. Note places that confuse you. Underline the main action or idea of each paragraph.

Next | Meet with your partner. Help each other find these words in the text.

yearned   adamant   detest   available   dumbfounded

Read the sentences around the words. Think about how they fit in the whole story. Define the words. Which key words or phrases from the text help you and your partner define them? One row is already filled in for you.

Word	What It Means	Key Words or Phrases
yearned		
adamant	firm, not willing to change one's mind	Brian's father says he will never permit it.
detest		
available		
dumbfounded		

Your Name: _____

Purr for the Perfect Pet *(cont.)*

Now   Answer the story questions below.

1. Why didn't Brian want a fish? _____

_____

2. Before Brian found the notice for the free cat, he suggested three animals that he would like to have as pets. Draw the three animals. Draw them in the order in which Brian asked for them. Below each drawing, write the animal's name.

First	Second	Third
_____	_____	_____

3. What did Brian's father like about a canary? _____

Give one reason why Brian's father didn't think it was fair to have a canary as a pet. Use a quotation to show your answer.

_____

_____

4. You are told in the first line that Brian's "heart ached." Why did the author say Brian's heart ached rather than his hand or head?

_____

_____

_____

5. Two of the following are kinds of rodents: **parrot**, **chipmunk**, **squirrel**, **eagle**. Pick which two you think are rodents. Defend your answer by evidence from the story.

The rodents from that list are the _____ and the _____.

The following parts from the story helped me answer this question: _____

_____

_____

Your Name: _____

Purr for the Perfect Pet *(cont.)*

Then   Reread the entire story one last time. Pay attention to how the last paragraph relates to the rest of the story.

6. Write a very short summary of the last paragraph.

_____

_____

7. What kind of pet do you think the author wanted you to think of when you read the title? Why?

_____

_____

How do you think the author wanted you to feel when you read the last paragraph? Tell why.

_____

_____

Would the ending have the same effect if the reader didn't know what a cheetah was? Why?

_____

_____

8. Write a short paragraph about someone who is dumbfounded. You can make up a character and a situation. Or, you can just write about a time when you were dumbfounded.

_____

_____

_____

_____

_____

Exchange papers with a partner. Discuss your stories. Tell your partner if you think he/she followed directions well and wrote about a person who was dumbfounded. Each partner should be able to defend his/her story.

Learn More   Use the Internet to listen to cheetah sounds. Find out other cheetah facts, too. Create a diagram or chart that shows how cheetahs' bodies are perfectly made to run fast. List at least four parts of a cheetah's body that are built for speed.

Boom!

 Boom! There was a huge explosion. Dirt and rock poured down. Parts of a tunnel collapsed. Men were trapped deep under Lake Erie, and they had no way to escape. Workers tried to rescue the men, but they could not. The rescue workers now needed rescuing!

 The year was 1916. The city of Cleveland needed clean water. Water close to the shore of Lake Erie was no longer clean enough for people to drink. To get cleaner water, people started to build a water-intake tunnel. The tunnel was 40 feet below the lake bed. It went for four miles toward the center of the lake. Disaster struck when natural gas vented up from the lake bed. Somehow the gas ignited when it flowed into the tunnel. It lit on fire and exploded.

 Two times rescue workers rushed in, but the air in the tunnel was too unsafe to breathe. It was filled with gas and smoke. Many of the rescue workers collapsed. They were no longer rescuers. They were in need of help, too! One member of the rescue team ran to Garrett Morgan's house. He pounded on Morgan's door and pleaded with him to come to the tunnel. He begged Morgan to come with some of his hoods.

 Morgan was the son of two former slaves. Morgan stopped going to school after the seventh grade, but he never stopped learning. He invented all kinds of things. One of his inventions was a safety hood. The hood kept one's eyes safe from smoke. It also had a series of air tubes that hung near the ground. Smoke rises, and the tubes let one breathe the cleaner air below the smoke.

 Morgan rushed to the tunnel. His brother came, too. Morgan was in his pajamas, but he had four hoods. Many of the rescuers did not trust the hoods, but Morgan and his brother went into the tunnel. Both of them emerged carrying victims on their backs. People saw first-hand the value of the hoods. Later, firefighters gave Morgan a special medal.

Your Name: _____   Partner: _____

Boom! *(cont.)*

First   Silently read "Boom!" You might see words you do not know. There might be parts you do not understand. Keep reading! Try to find out what the story is mainly about.

Then   Sum up the story. Write the main actions and most important information. If someone reads your summary, that person should know it is this story you are writing about.

_____

_____

_____

_____

_____

After That   Read the story again. Use a pencil to circle or mark words you don't know. Note places that confuse you. Underline the main action or idea of each paragraph.

Next   Meet with your partner, and find these words in the story.

Word	Paragraph #
vented	2
ignited	2
pleaded	3
emerged	5

Each partner should pick one word from the chart above.

a. My partner's chosen word is _____.

In this passage, this word must mean _____.

We think this because _____

_____

b. My chosen word is _____.

In this passage, this word must mean _____.

We think this because _____

_____

Your Name: _____

Boom! *(cont.)*

Now   Answer the story questions below.

1. Why did the tunnel collapse? _____

_____

2. Why did Morgan have tubes that hung near the ground on his hoods?

_____

_____

Do you think Morgan knew how smoke behaved before he made his hoods? Explain.

_____

_____

3. The author tells you that Morgan was wearing pajamas when he got to the tunnel. What might the author be trying to show us about Morgan and about what was happening?

_____

_____

Would it have been more or less effective if the author had just said, "Morgan rushed to the scene" instead of telling you that Morgan was still in his pajamas. Why or why not?

_____

_____

4. The passage tells us that a rescue worker ran to Morgan's house to get his help. Imagine that scene. Use the information you have been given. Imagine the conversation that must have taken place between the rescue worker and Morgan. Write that conversation here.

Use quotation marks to show that someone is speaking. To show the way someone is talking (excitedly, calmly) or what that person is doing (pounding on the door), use parentheses.

Worker: (pounding on door) _____

Morgan: (opening door) _____

Worker: _____

Morgan: _____

Worker: _____

Morgan: _____

Your Name: _____

Boom! *(cont.)*

Then Reread the entire story one last time.

5. The title of the passage was "Boom!" Do you think this was a good title for the passage? Tell why or why not.

_____

_____

6. Imagine the title of the passage was "Cleveland's Tunnel." Do you think this is a better title? Tell why or why not.

_____

_____

Think up a new title for the passage. Write it here: _____

Why would this be a good title for the passage? _____

_____

_____

7. You are told that at first many of the rescuers did not trust the hoods. When did they begin to trust them?

_____

_____

Do you think your opinion might change about something if you see it being used first-hand? Tell why you think so.

_____

_____

Learn More Find out more about another of Morgan's inventions. On another piece of paper, write a news article with information about Morgan and his invention. Your article should be one or two paragraphs. Include a headline that will make the reader want to read your article!

The Right Feet

 1 **Patti:** (*whining*) My feet hurt! That's the only reason I didn't win the race. Maybe I fractured a bone. There must be something broken, because the pain is terrible.

Hugo: (*consoling*) There, there. Don't feel bad that you lost. You tried your best. Keep practicing, and maybe you'll do better next time.

Patti: (*snapping*) Don't console me by telling me about next time. That's not comforting! I'm telling you, there's something wrong with my feet.

2 **Julie:** (*matter-of-factly*) I fractured my arm once when I fell off a swing. It really hurt. I had to wear a plaster cast for a month.

Patti: (*waspishly*) I don't care about your arm. I'm concerned with my feet! I'm telling you they really hurt.

Hugo: (*soothingly*) Try to calm down, Patti. Let me take a look.

3 *Hugo squats down and looks at Patti's feet.*

Julie: (*curiously*) Can you tell if anything is wrong?

Hugo: (*humorously*) Patti, I know what the problem is. Nothing is fractured. You just put your shoes on the wrong feet!

Patti: (*indignantly*) Don't be ridiculous! What a silly thing to say! I didn't put my shoes on the wrong feet. I didn't!

4 **Julie:** (*curiously*) Patti, why are you so indignant? You made a mistake, that's all. We all make mistakes and learn from them. So why be upset?

Patti: (*angrily*) I'm upset because you're not making sense! How can I put my shoes on the wrong feet? I only have two feet. I don't have any other feet, so of course I put my shoes on my own feet! You shouldn't be teasing me when I'm in pain!

5 **Hugo:** (*trying to keep the humor out of his voice*) Patti, we weren't teasing you. Of course you only have two feet. But you have a left foot and a right foot. You put your shoes on your own feet, but you put the left shoe on the right foot and the right shoe on the left foot!

Your Name: _____ Partner: _____

The Right Feet (cont.)

First Silently read "The Right Feet." You might see words you do not know. There might be parts you do not understand. Keep reading! Try to find out what the play is mainly about.

Then Sum up the play. Write about the main characters, actions, and most important information. If someone reads your summary, that person should know it is this play you are writing about, not a different one!

_____

_____

_____

_____

_____

After That Read the play again. Use a pencil to circle or mark words you don't know. Note places that confuse you. Underline the main action or idea of each paragraph.

Next Meet with your partner. Look at all the words in the parentheses that describe the characters' tone of voice when they are speaking. Use what the characters say to help you define the words. Then write a phrase or a sentence you might say if you were speaking with the same tone of voice. The first one is done for you.

Tone Words	What You Might Say
whining	I'm sick and tired of walking so much. I hate it!
consoling	
snapping	
matter-of-factly	
soothingly	
curiously	
humorously	
indignantly	
angrily	

Your Name: _____

The Right Feet (cont.)

Now   Answer the questions below.

1. Why did Patti think she might have fractured a bone?

_____

2. Why didn't Patti think her shoes were on the wrong feet?

_____

_____

3. In the play, Patti speaks waspishly to Julie. Write down what you think Patti's voice sounded like when she spoke waspishly.

_____

What do you think of when you think of a real, live wasp? In the box, draw a picture of a wasp. On the lines, tell how this image helps you know how Patti's voice sounded.

_____

_____

_____

_____

4. Imagine you can't find your key, but it turns out that you have just put it in a different pocket than you usually do. Imagine you are asking Hugo, Patti, and Julie to help you find the key. What do you think each of these characters might say to you as you try to find it? Explain.

Character	What He/She Would Say	Why You Think This
Hugo		
Patti		
Julie		

Your Name: _____

The Right Feet (cont.)

Then   Reread the entire play one last time.

5. In the play, the author presents a problem.

   a. What is the problem? _____

   b. What is the solution to the problem? _____

   c. Is the problem fixed in the play? Why or why not? _____

   _____

   d. At what point in the story are you given the information needed to fix the problem?

   _____

6. How does the author make you think the problem might be a broken foot bone?

   _____

   _____

   _____

7. Look back at the play. Why does the author include the words in parentheses? What information do these words give you? How would the play be different without them?

   _____

   _____

   _____

   _____

Learn More   Look up shoe facts. See if you can find five interesting facts about the history of shoes. Perhaps you can find out when they started making right and left shoes!

   Fact #1: _____

   Fact #2: _____

   Fact #3: _____

   Fact #4: _____

   Fact #5: _____

A Finger Where?

 Games are for entertaining. They are played for amusement. One amusing game involves fingers. Each player puts a finger in the other player's nose. Then, the players swing back and forth, keeping their fingers in each other's nose.

 Another amusing game involves hair. Both males and females like to play this game. In the game, one player bites the hair off of the other player's face! Then the two players take turns passing the clump of hair between them. How do the players exchange the clump of hair? They use their teeth! Each time the clump is passed, a little hair drops off. The game is over when the hair runs out.

 Who exactly would play such games? Who could find these games entertaining? Who would enjoy sticking a finger up someone else's nose? Who likes biting off someone's facial hair? It is not a person! It is an animal called the capuchin monkey.

 These monkeys live in Central and South America. They are small, with bodies anywhere from 12 to 22 inches long. They have tails, too, and their tails are as long as their bodies. They are gregarious. This means they are social animals that like living in groups. They eat, play, and sleep together.

 People learn by observation. Capuchins learn by watching, too. Young capuchins see older capuchins bite the top off of the fruit of the palm nut. They see the adults suck out the fruit juice. Then they watch the adults discard the rest of the fruit with the nut still inside. Later, when the fruit has dried, the young monkeys watch the adults gather up the discarded fruits. The adults take the dried fruits to a place where there are big stones. There, the adults pick up the stones and smash the fruits. The adults crack open the fruits so they can get to the nut inside. It takes young monkeys about eight years to learn how to do this.

Your Name: _____   Partner: _____

A Finger Where? *(cont.)*

First   Silently read "A Finger Where?" You might see words you do not know. There might be parts you do not understand. Keep reading! Try to find out what the story is mainly about.

Then   Sum up the story. Write the main actions and most important information. If someone reads your summary, that person should know it is this story you are writing about.

_____

_____

_____

_____

_____

After That   Read the story again. Use a pencil to circle or mark words you don't know. Note places that confuse you. Underline the main action or idea of each paragraph.

Next   Meet with your partner. Help each other find these words in the text.

     amusement   exchange   facial   gregarious   discarded

Read the sentences around the words. Think about how they fit in the whole story. Define the words. Which key words or phrases from the text helped you define them?

Word	Definition	Key Words or Phrases
amusement	something fun or entertaining	The monkeys play the games for amusement and entertainment.
exchange		
facial		
gregarious		
discarded		

Your Name: _____

A Finger Where? (cont.)

Now   Answer the story questions below.

1. What does the monkey do after it has put a finger in the other monkey's nose?

_____

2. In inches, about how long is a capuchin monkey's tail? _____

Explain how you were able to figure this out. _____

_____

_____

_____

3. Would a gregarious person be more likely to swim with friends or swim alone?

_____

Defend your answer using evidence from the story.

_____

_____

_____

4. Write down two things the young monkeys observe the adult monkeys doing *after* the discarded fruit has dried.

_____

_____

_____

_____

_____

_____

_____

_____

Your Name: _____

A Finger Where? *(cont.)*

Then) Reread the entire story one last time. Pay attention to when you first learn who is playing the games.

5. Write a brief summary (not more than a few words or one sentence) of **each** paragraph that comes **before** the paragraph in which you find out the story is about capuchin monkeys.

_____

_____

_____

6. Why do you think the author waited to let the reader find out who was playing the games?

_____

_____

Was the writer giving you a hint about who was playing the game when she wrote, "Both males and females like to play this game. In the game, one player bites the hair off of another player's face!" Is this a hint? Explain.

_____

_____

_____

7. You are told that young monkeys watch adults for about eight years before they learn how to get to the palm nut. Think of something that you learned by observation. Tell what you learned and about how long it took. Compare and contrast your experience with that of a young capuchin monkey.

_____

_____

_____

_____

Learn More) Find out if capuchin monkeys are *diurnal* or *nocturnal*. Also, find out if they are *arboreal*. On a separate piece of paper, create an illustrated glossary that uses words and drawings to define these three terms. In your glossary, explain how these words relate to capuchin monkeys.

When Morning Is Afternoon

 Ben said, "I'm glad my meeting is at two o'clock on Monday. I will have time to eat lunch and go over my notes. It is an important meeting, and I want to be prepared. I will be alert, too, because I won't be tired."

 Lizzy said, "I'm rejoicing because my meeting is at 11 o'clock on Monday. I'm glad it is just before lunch. I should not be tired at that time. I'm usually very alert in the late morning, and that is why it is the best time to have a meeting."

 "That's right," Aya said after checking her schedule. "I have a meeting Monday night at eight o'clock. I'll eat a light dinner first, and then I'll study my notes. I want to be prepared."

 Yuki said, "I am afraid that I will not be alert at my next meeting. Who scheduled this meeting? How did they pick such an inconvenient time? My meeting is Tuesday at three in the morning! Three in the morning is not a convenient time for me. I should be asleep! I hope I'm not too exhausted."

 Ben, Lizzy, Aya, and Yuki all went to their scheduled meetings. They all used computers to communicate. They could see each other and talk to each other. It was a different time for each of them, but they were all at the same meeting at the same instant!

 Earth rotates. It spins. It takes one day, or 24 hours, to make a complete rotation. Earth is divided into time zones because it can't be day everywhere on Earth at the same time. When the sun shines on one side of Earth, it doesn't shine on the other. The time zones help us communicate. They help us do business. They help us know where it is morning, noon, or night.

 Ben was in Washington, DC, the capital of the United States. Lizzy was in the state of Oregon. Aya was in Egypt. Yuki was in Japan. Oregon's time is three hours behind Washington, DC. Egypt's time is six hours ahead of Washington, DC's time. Japan's time is 13 hours ahead!

Your Name: _____   Partner: _____

When Morning Is Afternoon *(cont.)*

First) Silently read "When Morning Is Afternoon." You might see words you do not know and read parts you do not understand. Keep reading! Find out what the story is mainly about.

Then) Sum up the story. Write the main actions and most important information. If someone reads your summary, that person should know it is this story you are writing about.

_____

_____

_____

_____

_____

After That) Read the story again. Use a pencil to circle or mark words you don't know. Note places that confuse you. Underline the main action or idea of each paragraph.

Next) Meet with your partner. Help each other find these words in the text.

   alert   rejoicing   inconvenient   convenient

Read the sentences around the words to help you figure out what they mean. Then answer the questions below.

   a. Why is it good to be **alert** in school or in a meeting?

   _____

   b. Would you be **rejoicing** today if you got to pet a snake?

   _____

   _____

   c. Would it be **inconvenient** to have a lion as a pet? Give one reason why or why not.

   _____

   _____

   d. What animal would make a **convenient** pet? Give one reason why.

   _____

   _____

Your Name: _____

When Morning Is Afternoon *(cont.)*

Now Answer the story questions below.

1. For each character, the meeting took place at a different time. Draw hands on the clocks below each character's name. Show the time that the meeting began for that character.

Aya	Ben	Lizzy	Yuki

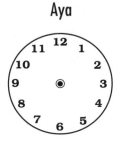 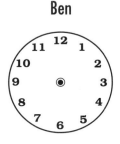 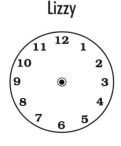 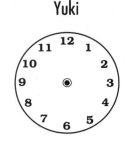

2. Who was meeting on Tuesday instead of Monday? _____

Why was the meeting on Tuesday instead of Monday for this person?

_____

_____

_____

3. Why is Earth divided into time zones? Find this information in the story. Use your own words to explain this information. Don't copy the words from the story.

_____

_____

_____

4. Whose meeting was at the most convenient time? _____

Explain why you think this. _____

_____

_____

Who is the least likely person to have scheduled the meeting? _____

Use words and phrases from the passage to defend your answer.

_____

_____

Your Name: _____

When Morning Is Afternoon *(cont.)*

Then Reread the entire story one last time.

5. What do you find out in paragraph 5? _____

_____

_____

6. Why do you think the author waited until paragraph 5 before giving this information?

_____

_____

_____

7. Imagine that the author had started the story with paragraph 6. How would this have changed the story? Do you think it would have made it better? Tell why or why not.

_____

_____

_____

_____

Learn More Pick out five countries on a globe. For each country, type into a search engine, "What time is it in *[name of country]*." Complete the chart below to show the time difference between these countries and the place where you live.

Name of Country	Time Now	Your Time	Difference in Hours

Life-Saving Haircut

 Think of the word *rescue*. The sound of a fire engine's siren might come to mind. Think *help*, and one might think of a speeding ambulance. Think of the word *aid*, and one might think of a lifeguard throwing a ring into the water. One might think of all these things when it comes to saving lives, but it isn't likely one would think of a haircut. As unlikely as it seems, all it took to save Chris was a haircut. If Chris had not been given a haircut, it is believed he would have died in just a few weeks.

 Chris was first seen by a hiker. The hiker was in the Australian bush. The hiker saw kangaroos hopping, but then he saw Chris. At first he didn't know what Chris was. Chris is a sheep, but he didn't look like any sheep the hiker had ever seen. Chris looked like nothing but a mammoth ball of filthy wool.

 Sheep are raised in Australia for their wool. These type of sheep must be sheared regularly. So, they are sheared annually, or once a year. Somehow, Chris had wandered off and lived on his own for five or six years. For all those years, Chris missed his annual shearing.

 Chris's wool had grown to about four to five times the normal amount. He was almost blinded by the wool flopping into his eyes. His hooves were damaged from carrying the weight of all the extra wool. He was easy prey for dingoes (wild dogs) because he could hardly move. If he had fallen, he would not have been able to get up.

 Chris's haircut set a sheep-shearing record. Over 89 pounds of wool was cut away! Chris was a lot lighter after being sheared. His weight had been cut in half! Today, Chris might not be able to hop as far as a kangaroo, but he is quick and nimble. His hooves have recovered, and with his healthy feet, he is no longer easy prey. If a dingo comes after him, he can run away!

Your Name: _____ Partner: _____

Life-Saving Haircut (cont.)

First Silently read "Life-Saving Haircut." You might see words you do not know. There might be parts you do not understand. Keep reading! Try to find out what the story is mainly about.

Then Sum up the story. Write the main actions and most important information. If someone reads your summary, that person should know it is this story you are writing about.

_____

_____

_____

_____

_____

After That Read the story again. Use a pencil to circle or mark words you don't know. Note places that confuse you. Underline the main action or idea of each paragraph.

Next Meet with your partner. Help each other find these words in the text.

    aid   mammoth   annual   hooves   nimble

Decide with your partner what these words mean. Each partner should record this information on his/her chart. (See below.) Together, make up new sentences that use these words correctly. Write these on your charts, too. When you are done, check each other's work to make sure everything is spelled correctly and no words are missing.

Word	Definition	New Sentence
aid		
mammoth		
annual		
hooves		
nimble		

Your Name: _____

Life-Saving Haircut *(cont.)*

Now   Answer the story questions below.

1. Why was Chris's hair so long? _____

_____

2. How does the author describe Chris's appearance **before** his haircut?

Quote the last line of paragraph 2 here.

Draw a picture of this description.

_____

_____

_____

_____

3. What happened to Chris's weight after his haircut?

_____

Imagine you weighed 200 pounds. If you were like Chris, how much would you weigh **after** your haircut? Support your answer by quoting or referring to words in the story.

_____

_____

_____

4. Another word for *scissors* is *shears*. In this case, *shears* is a noun. How does the noun *shears* differ from the verb *shear*? When you explain, use examples from the story.

_____

_____

_____

5. Tell why it is important for some sheep to be sheared. Use information from the story.

_____

_____

_____

_____

Your Name: _____

Life-Saving Haircut *(cont.)*

Then   Reread the entire story one last time. Think about how paragraph 1 relates to the rest of the story.

6. Write a very short summary of paragraph 1. What happens? What information are you given about Chris?

_____

_____

7. Why do you think the author waited until later in the story to tell you what kind of an animal Chris is?

_____

_____

8. The author could have started the story a different way. The story could have begun like this: *Chris was in danger.* Write a sentence that could follow the new first line. It is up to you to decide if you are going to say if Chris is a sheep or not!

   Chris was in danger. _____

_____

_____

9. In writing, the term *tone* refers to the author's feelings, thoughts, or opinions about the subject of her writing. What do you think the author's tone is in "Life-Saving Haircut"? How does she seem to feel about Chris and his problem? Use an example or two to support your opinion about the author's tone.

_____

_____

_____

_____

Learn More   Use the Internet to locate a "before" and an "after" picture of Chris. Find out some facts about the wool industry. What is wool used for? What makes wool special?

Key Search Terms	
◆ Chris	◆ Australia
◆ sheep	◆ shearing

Riddles and More Riddles

 Ms. Boggle smiled at her class. "I'm always telling you that I don't ever want to hear you say 'No, I can't do it.'" The students in Ms. Boggle's class all nodded in agreement. They knew that Ms. Boggle wanted them to say something like, "I'm having trouble learning how to do this," or "I need some help so I can understand this better." Ms. Boggle felt those statements showed a better attitude than, "No, I can't do it."

 "But there is one thing you can't say yes to! You can't do it! It's impossible!" As Ms. Boggle said these words, a smile as wide as a mile crossed her face. "Does anyone know what you can't say yes to?"

 The students were perplexed. They didn't know what the answer was. Everyone laughed when Ms. Boggle told them the answer. No one could say yes to the question, "Are you asleep?"

 "Here are two more perplexing riddles," Ms. Boggle said. "They're puzzling, but perhaps you can figure them out. You're all smart, so I don't think you will find them baffling at all! First, how do you make the word *one* disappear? Second, what word do students always spell incorrectly?"

 The class was confused for a little while, but then everyone solved the riddles. The way to make the word *one* disappear was to put a *g* in front of it. Put a *g* in front of *one*, and it makes the word *gone*! As to what word was always spelled incorrectly, it was the word *incorrectly*! If you spelled the word *incorrectly* correctly, you had to spell it i-n-c-o-r-r-e-c-t-l-y!

 After lunch, the class told Ms. Boggle they had a riddle for her. They warned her that she would be perplexed, and then they asked her, "What can be opened but can't be closed?" Ms. Boggle was baffled at first, but then she clapped her hands in glee. "I know it," she said merrily. "The answer is an egg! You can open an egg, but you can't close it."

Your Name: _____ Partner: _____

Riddles and More Riddles *(cont.)*

First Silently read "Riddles and More Riddles." You might see words you do not know and read parts you do not understand. Keep reading! Find out what the story is mainly about.

Then Sum up the story. Write the main actions and most important information. If someone reads your summary, that person should know it is this story you are writing about.

_____

_____

_____

_____

_____

_____

After That Read the story again. Use a pencil to circle or mark words you don't know. Note places that confuse you. Underline the main action or idea of each paragraph.

Next Meet with your partner. Help each other find these words in the text.

perplexed   baffled   glee

Read the sentences around the words. Think about how they fit in the whole story. Decide what the words mean.

Two of the words are synonyms. *Synonyms* are words that mean nearly the same thing. Complete the following statements.

a. The two synonyms are _____ and _____.

These words mean _____.

Here is how the story helped me to know this: _____

_____

Next, write down two synonyms for the other word. Complete these statements.

b. The other word is _____.

Two synonyms for this word are _____ and _____.

I know this because _____

_____

Your Name: _____

Riddles and More Riddles (cont.)

Now   Answer the story questions below.

1. What might a student say to Ms. Boggle if he or she didn't know how to do a math problem? Quote some words from the story as part of your answer.

_____

_____

2. Why do you think Ms. Boggle doesn't want to hear "No, I can't do it"?

_____

_____

3. In paragraph 2, it says that a smile "as wide as a mile" crossed Ms. Boggle's face. Can one really smile as wide as a mile? Why or why not?

_____

_____

Why do you think the author used this phrase to describe Ms. Boggle's smile? What do you think the author wanted you to understand?

_____

_____

_____

4. When Ms. Boggle thinks of the answer to this riddle, what might she do with her hands? Imagine she is given the riddle, "What can you catch but not throw?"

  When Ms. Boggle realizes the answer is a "cold," she might _____

_____

Why do you think Ms. Boggle will react this way? Use evidence from the story to support your answer.

_____

_____

Your Name: _____

Riddles and More Riddles *(cont.)*

Then Reread the entire story one last time.

5. If you only read the first paragraph, why might you think the story has the wrong title?

_____

_____

_____

6. Did the title help you want to keep reading? Why or why not?

_____

_____

7. Which of the following riddles do *you* think is the most perplexing?

    a. What is something that you can take from and then it will get bigger?

    b. There is something in my pocket, but my pocket is empty. What is it?

The answer to both riddles is "a hole."

Explain why one of these riddles might baffle someone.

_____

_____

_____

_____

Learn More One of the oldest riddles was written down almost 4,000 years ago. It is a riddle from the ancient civilization of Sumer. The riddle goes: "There is a house. One enters it blind and comes out seeing. What is it?" The answer is "a school." What do you think this riddle and answer could tell you about the Sumerians?

_____

_____

_____

_____

The Amazing World of Ants

 Ants are a lot more than pests that invade a picnic. They are amazing insects. Ants have colonized almost every landmass in the world. The only places they don't live are on a few remote islands and on Antarctica, which is easily the world's most inhospitable continent.

 There are many different kinds of ants. One kind of ant lives in Africa. It is called the driver ant. The driver ant is a kind of army ant. People have used this ant to stitch up gashes! They use the ants to staple their cuts shut! How would one do such a thing? First, carefully pick up the ant. Then hold its mouth with its powerful jaws to the wounded area. Get the ant to bite on both sides of the gash. The last thing to do is break off the ant's body. The head remains, and the ant's pincer-like jaws act as staples. They are strong enough to hold the cut together for days.

 The leafcutter ant is another kind of ant. These ants live in South and Central America. Some of their colonies have as many as 8 million ants! These ants march in a convoy. They are safer in a convoy because they can protect each other. As a group, they cut and collect fresh leaves. Once they get the leaves back to their colony, they chew them up and spit them out. They fertilize them with their dung before adding them to the top of their garden. The ants carefully tend their garden. They groom it, weed it, and cut out the bad parts. What grows in their garden? It is a special fungus that the ants eat.

 The bulldog ant of Australia is fierce. You don't want this ant coming to a picnic! Scientists have cut this ant in two. When they do, there is a fierce battle. The head seizes the tail in its teeth. The tail defends itself bravely by stinging the head! Sometimes the head and tail will fight for over an hour!

Your Name: _____   Partner: _____

The Amazing World of Ants *(cont.)*

First   Silently read "The Amazing World of Ants." You might see words you do not know and read parts you do not understand. Keep reading! Find out what the story is mainly about.

Then   Sum up the story. Write the main actions and most important information. If someone reads your summary, that person should know it is this story you are writing about.

_____

_____

_____

_____

_____

_____

_____

After That   Read the story again. Use a pencil to circle or mark words you don't know. Note places that confuse you. Underline the main action or idea of each paragraph.

Next   Meet with your partner. Help each other find these words in the text.

remote   inhospitable

Before you write what these words might mean, think and talk! Reread the part that tells you where ants *don't* live. Discuss the following before completing the chart below:

a. Would it be easy for an ant to get to an island in the middle of the ocean? Why or why not?

b. Is it easy to live in Antarctica? Why or why not?

Now write down what you think these words mean.

Word	Meaning	Why You Think This
remote		
inhospitable		

Your Name: _____

The Amazing World of Ants (cont.)

Now Answer the story questions below.

1. At what times might the driver ant *not* be a pest? Use facts from the story in your answer.

   _____

   _____

2. When leafcutter ants go out to get leaves, do they go out alone or with other ants?

   _____

   Find a quote from the story to support your answer. _____

   _____

3. In the story, what kind of ant is described as fierce? _____

   This kind of ant has powerful jaws so why do you think people don't use it as a staple to hold cuts together?

   _____

   _____

   _____

4. The story tells us that leafcutter ants grow gardens. People also grow gardens. From the story, find two ways that these ants' gardens are similar to people's gardens. Find one way that they are different. Complete the diagram.

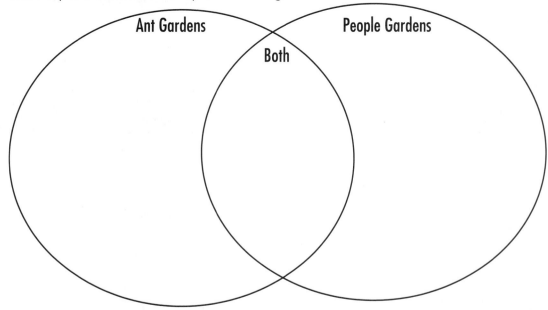

Your Name: _____

The Amazing World of Ants (cont.)

Then | Reread the entire story one last time. Pay attention to the structure of the story.

5. The story starts with an introductory paragraph. The next three paragraphs are examples.
   Write a short conclusion to the story.

   _____

   _____

   _____

   _____

6. Do you think a conclusion was needed? Would it have made the story better in some way?
   Give at least one reason why or why not. (There is no right or wrong answer. It's your
   opinion!)

   _____

   _____

   _____

7. Out of the three examples of ants, which one do *you* find the most amazing? Tell why. Use
   examples from the story to show why this type of ant is so amazing.

   _____

   _____

   _____

   _____

Learn More | Use the Internet or books to find pictures of different kinds of ants. Find out what the
different kinds of ants eat. Divide a page into four sections. In each section, create a small
menu for a different type of ant.

Nothing New to Invent

 "It's so unfair," Rose said in a peevish voice. "How can we invent something? Everything has already been invented!" Rose looked around the room. "And now I'm peeved at April and A.J.," she said. "Where are they? They were going to come and help me with my task. They were going to help me think of something to invent. They're probably relaxing on an ocean-sofa."

 Luke said, "It's more likely that they're racing around on a dino-rider. Now that was a great invention! I love riding around on my dino-rider! I always put it in the T-Rex mode. Then I sit on its head!"

"I wish the ocean-sofa or the dino-rider had never been invented," Rose said wistfully. "Then we could invent them!"

 "'To invent, you need a good imagination and a pile of junk,'" Luke said and then was silent for a moment. In a wistful voice, he said, "That's a great quote. I wish I had said it first, but I didn't. Thomas Alva Edison said it."

"Thomas Alva Edison?" Rose asked. "Didn't he invent the light bulb?"

"Yes," Luke nodded. "He invented lots of other things, too. He had patents for over 1,000 inventions."

 "See?" Rose said, exasperated. "What's left to invent?" She made another cry of frustration, but it quickly turned to surprise. April and A.J. were suddenly standing in front of her! They appeared out of thin air!

"We've been here all the time," April said.

When Rose protested that it wasn't possible, A.J. explained. "We invented a cloak of invisibility. Here, Luke, you try it."

 Rose gasped when Luke suddenly seemed to disappear. Then her face lit up. It was as if a light bulb had turned on. "I've got it!" she cried. "I know what I can invent! I can invent a story! My story is going to be about a cloak that makes people invisible!"

Your Name: _____   Partner: _____

Nothing New to Invent (cont.)

First Silently read "Nothing New to Invent." You might see words you do not know. There might be parts you do not understand. Keep reading! FInd out what the story is mainly about.

Then Sum up the story. Write the main actions and most important information. If someone reads your summary, that person should know it is this story you are writing about.

_____

_____

_____

_____

_____

_____

_____

After That Read the story again. Use a pencil to circle or mark words you don't know. Note places that confuse you. Underline the main action or idea of each paragraph.

Next Meet with your partner. Help each other find these words in the text.

   peevish   *wistfully*   *exasperated*   *frustration*

Decide together which three of these words might fit with how you feel when you are irritated or bothered. For each word, tell which part of the story helped you decide.

Word	Part of the Story

Which word might fit with how you feel when you wish something or long for something? Tell which part of the story helped you decide.

Word	Part of the Story

Your Name: _____

Nothing New to Invent *(cont.)*

Now   Answer the story questions below.

1. Why did Rose think it was unfair that she had to invent something?

_____

2. What were the two inventions that Rose and Luke thought April and A.J. might be using?

_____

Pick one of the inventions from your answer above. In the box, draw a picture of it. On the lines, write two sentences describing how it works or what you can do with it.

_____

_____

_____

_____

_____

_____

3. The last paragraph contains the following sentence: "It was as if a light bulb had turned on." What does this mean? Did a light bulb really light up? Explain.

_____

_____

_____

Why do you think the author used this expression, "a light bulb turned on"? Refer to Thomas Edison in your answer.

_____

_____

_____

4. Decide if this story is fact or fiction. Then use evidence from the story to prove it.

_____

_____

_____

Your Name: _____

Nothing New to Invent (cont.)

Then   Reread the entire story one last time. Think about how there is a problem and a solution.

5. Sum up Rose's problem. Then tell what her solution is.

_____

_____

_____

6. Why do you think the author waited until the end to tell you Rose's solution?

_____

_____

Do you think it was good solution? Why or why not? (There is no right or wrong answer here. It is what you think!)

_____

_____

_____

7. Remember Edison's quote: "To invent, you need a good imagination and a pile of junk." Now rewrite the last two lines of the story.

I can invent a _____!

My _____

_____!"

Learn More   Find out more about Thomas Alva Edison, other inventors, or an invention. Write a few sentences about what you learned about the inventor or the invention.

_____

_____

_____

_____

Insult or Compliment?

 Some people think it is bad to be called a birdbrain. They think it is an insult, and they think they are being called stupid. Someone called me a birdbrain, but I did not feel bad. I did not take it as an insult. I took it as a compliment! I know I am smart.

 Think of an analogy as a kind of puzzle. An analogy is a comparison between two things. The things are alike, but only in one way.

> Here is one example: *dog* is to *bark* as *cat* is to meow.
> Here is another: *house* is to *person* as *nest* is to *bird*.

The word pairs *dog and bark* are like *cat and meow* because they both match an animal with its sound. The word pairs *person and house* and *bird and nest* both match something to where it lives. Think about the words *hot* and *cold*. *Hot* and *cold* are opposites. An analogy for this word pair could be *hard* is to *soft* or *big* is to *small*.

 Why do people feel insulted if they are called a birdbrain? Birds have very small brains, and so people think birds aren't intelligent. When people are called birdbrains, they think they are being told they are not smart. The truth is that some birds are very intelligent!

 You have to be smart to solve puzzles. You have to use your brain power. When you solve an analogy, you have to use a lot of brain power. You have to really think hard. Scientists have taught crows to solve analogies! If a crow is shown a card with AA, it can be taught to pick a card that shows BB or CC. It doesn't pick a card that shows AB or BC.

 I don't waste my brain power on getting upset when someone insults me or calls me a birdbrain. I think about puzzles instead. I puzzle over how to turn an insult into a compliment, and, just like smart birds, I solve analogies!

Your Name: _____ Partner: _____

Insult or Compliment? *(cont.)*

First Silently read "Insult or Compliment?" You might see words you do not know. There might be parts you do not understand. Keep reading! Find out what the story is mainly about.

Then Sum up the story. Write the main actions and most important information. If someone reads your summary, that person should know it is this story you are writing about.

_____

_____

_____

_____

_____

_____

After That Read the story again. Use a pencil to circle or mark words you don't know. Note places that confuse you. Underline the main action or idea of each paragraph.

Next Meet with your partner. Practice making analogies together.

   a. *wet* is to *dry* as _____ is to _____

   How are the word pairs alike? _____

   _____

   b. *mittens* are to *hands* as _____ are to _____

   How are the word pairs alike? _____

   _____

   c. *smart* is to *intelligent* as _____ is to _____

   How are the word pairs alike? _____

   _____

   d. *insult* is to *compliment* as _____ is to _____

   How are the word pairs alike? _____

   _____

Your Name: _____

Insult or Compliment? *(cont.)*

Now) Answer the story questions below.

1. What happened when someone called the author a birdbrain?

_____

_____

2. Some people might not feel the same as the author if they were called a birdbrain. How might they feel?

_____

_____

Why might they feel this way? Use information from the text in your answer.

_____

_____

_____

3. In the last paragraph, the author uses the word *puzzles* and *puzzle*. Go back and reread the sentences with the words *puzzles* and *puzzle*. How do the words *puzzles* and *puzzle* differ in usage and meaning?

_____

_____

_____

4. Imagine a trained crow is shown this card ➝ FG

The trained crow is then shown the following cards:

HH   II   HI

Based on the story, what card do you think the crow will pick? (Circle the correct card.)

Why?_____

_____

_____

Your Name: _____

Insult or Compliment? *(cont.)*

Then Reread the entire passage one last time.

5. Write a very short summary of paragraph 2. _____

_____

_____

Do you think the author would have included paragraph 2 if the crows had learned how to solve a different kind of puzzle? Explain why you think so.

_____

_____

_____

6. Is this story written in the first-person point of view? (If a story is written in first-person, it is as if a character is telling the story or talking to the reader. The character uses the pronouns "I" and "we.") Explain how you know. Use a direct quotation in your answer.

_____

_____

_____

7. Do you think the author would stop writing stories if you insulted the way she wrote the story? Tell why or why not.

_____

_____

_____

Learn More Find a copy of Aesop's Fable of "The Crow and the Pitcher." (There are many versions in book form or online for free.) Is the crow a good puzzle solver or a poor one?

_____

_____

_____

Mouse Feelings

1   "Aaagghh!" Cesar yelled when he saw a mouse run in front of him. "I hate mice. I detest them. I loathe them. There is nothing good or nice about mice or any other kind of varmint. They are useless pests. I wish they would all disappear. I really dislike them a lot."

2   "When I see something that I detest, I try to think of something that I like. What do you like, Cesar?" Bella asked.

3   Cesar thought for a moment. He said, "I don't loathe dogs. In fact, I feel the opposite. I really like them. It doesn't matter what kind it is. I like them if they're big or small, pretty or ugly, mixed mutt or purebred. Any kind of canine is the animal for me."

4   Cesar and Bella's conversation was suddenly interrupted by Dakota. "You've got to watch this," Dakota said as he held up his phone. It showed a video of a reporter. The three children watched and listened.

5   "Five weeks ago, a one-year-old dog named Tuna fell off a fishing boat. Tuna's owner reported her missing. He spent days looking for her. After a failed search, Tuna was presumed dead, as the closest land was a deserted island two miles away.

6   "Less than one hour ago, Tuna was found! She was skinny and a bit malnourished, but otherwise fine. With proper food and nourishment, she should quickly regain her health. Good thing this dog can dog paddle!"

7   "But if the island was deserted, what did Tuna eat?" Bella wondered aloud. "No one can survive five weeks without eating, so what did Tuna eat?" Bella's question was answered as the reporter continued to speak.

8   "Tuna was more than a great swimmer. She was one lucky canine, too. If there hadn't been mice on the island, Tuna would have starved to death. Somehow she caught enough of the tiny animals to stay alive."

Your Name: _____ Partner: _____

Mouse Feelings (cont.)

First Silently read "Mouse Feelings." You might see words you do not know. There might be parts you do not understand. Keep reading! Try to find out what the story is mainly about.

Then Sum up the story. Write the main actions and most important information. If someone reads your summary, that person should know it is this story you are writing about.

_____

_____

_____

_____

_____

_____

After That Read the story again. Use a pencil to circle or mark words you don't know. Note places that confuse you. Underline the main action or idea of each paragraph.

Next Meet with your partner. Help each other find these words in the text.

presumed   loathe   detest

Read the sentences around the words. Think about how they fit in the whole story. Define the words. The first one is done for you. Also, write the key words or phrases from the text that helped you define the words.

Word	Definition	Key Words or Phrases
presumed	thought to be, or believed	
loathe		
detest		

Think of two words that mean the opposite of *loathe* and *detest*.

1. _____   2. _____

Your Name: _____

Mouse Feelings *(cont.)*

Now   Answer the story questions below.

1. How did Cesar and Bella learn about Tuna? _____

_____

2. How did Tuna survive? _____

_____

3. Look at the two drawings below. Which one is more likely to show what Tuna looked like when she was found on the island, **Drawing A** or **Drawing B**?   Fill in the bubble beside your answer.

Ⓐ

Ⓑ

Why did you choose this drawing? Explain why it would fit the story better.

_____

_____

_____

_____

_____

_____

4. Do you think Cesar would like a poodle? _____

Defend your answer by quoting from the story. _____

_____

_____

5. How do you think the people who found Tuna on the island felt when they found her? Tell why you think so.

_____

_____

_____

_____

Your Name: _____

Mouse Feelings *(cont.)*

Then Reread the entire story one last time. Pay attention to how the first part of the story differs from the last part.

6. The first part of the story is mainly about _____.

_____

The last part of the story is mainly about _____.

_____

7. Cesar says, "There is nothing good or nice about mice or any other kind of varmint." Do you think Cesar felt the same at the end of the story? Tell why.

_____

_____

_____

8. This passage contains eight paragraphs. Which of these paragraphs contain words that are spoken by someone other than Cesar, Bella, or Dakota? Circle every number that names such a paragraph.

1   2   3   4   5   6   7   8

How do you know who is speaking in these paragraphs you have circled? What does the author do to help you understand who is speaking?

_____

_____

_____

Learn More Think of how the prefix *mal* changed the meaning of the word *nourished*.

nourished ➜ malnourished

Now figure out the meanings of the words *malpractice* and *malformed*.

Word	Meaning	How I Know This
malpractice		
malformed		

Down It Goes!

1 You are sick. You are so ill that you must go to the doctor. The doctor prescribes medicine. However, the medicine is not a liquid. You cannot drink it, and it doesn't taste like bubble gum or green apples. That's because the doctor wrote a prescription for pills. The problem is that you loathe pills. You hate them because you can't swallow them! It's a traumatic experience because they never go down!

2 Your parents have tried hiding pills in food. They have tried crushing them and mixing them in ice cream. They have even tried bribing you! They have told you they will pay you a dime for every pill you swallow!

3 You gag. You cough. You try to swallow, but the pills won't go down. You don't want them caught in your throat, so you hide them! You pretend to take them! That isn't good because you need to take the prescribed amount.

4 A doctor named Walter Haefeli wanted to make sure his patients took all their pills. He wanted to make the experience more pleasant and less traumatic. He did research, and after asking questions and doing tests on 150 people who had trouble taking pills, he wrote a paper. He found that the lean-forward technique made it easier for a lot of people to swallow pills.

5 First, you put the pill on your tongue. Next, you take a medium sip of water. Then you lean your head forward as you swallow. This technique works because when you tilt your head forward, the pill moves toward your throat.

6 You may loathe pills and hate taking medicine, but the truth is that sometimes you just have to. You can't hide your medicine even if you find swallowing pills to be a traumatic and scary experience. Life may not be all bubble gum and green apples, but perhaps you can try this technique next time you must take a pill.

Your Name: _____ Partner: _____

Down It Goes! *(cont.)*

First   Silently read "Down It Goes!" You might see words you do not know. There might be parts you do not understand. Keep reading! Try to find out what the story is mainly about.

Then   Sum up the story. Write the main actions and most important information. If someone reads your summary, that person should know it is this story you are writing about.

_____

_____

_____

_____

_____

After That   Read the story again. Use a pencil to circle or mark words you don't know. Note places that confuse you. Underline the main action or idea of each paragraph.

Next   Meet with your partner. Help each other find these words in the text.

     prescribes   *prescription*   *loathe*   *traumatic*   *technique*

Read the sentences around the words. Think about how they fit in the whole story. Define the words. Write down key words or phrases from the text that help you and your partner define them. The first row is filled in for you.

Word	Definition	Key Words or Phrases
prescribes	says you should take	The doctor prescribes medicine when you are sick.
prescription		
loathe		
traumatic		
technique		

Your Name: _____

Down It Goes! *(cont.)*

Now   Answer the story questions below.

1. Why are some people upset when their doctor writes a prescription for pills?

   _____

   _____

2. When the parents tried bribing, what did they do?

   _____

   _____

   Do you think the bribe would work better if the parents paid five dollars for every pill swallowed? Tell why or why not.

   _____

   _____

3. Why might the lean-forward technique be better than bribery? Use evidence from the story in your answer.

   _____

   _____

   _____

4. Do you think the author thinks most people like bubble gum and green apple flavors? Defend your answer using evidence from the story.

   _____

   _____

Which flavors do you think are best for medicine? Which would be the worst?

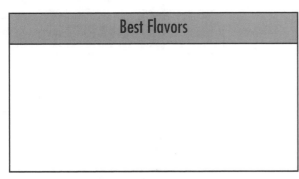

Best Flavors	Worst Flavors

Your Name: _____

Down It Goes! *(cont.)*

Then   Reread the entire story one last time.

5. Find the paragraph that describes the lean-forward technique. Write down the steps. Start each step with a verb.

Step #1 ➔   Put _____

Step #2 ➔   _____

Step #3 ➔   _____

6. Reread what you wrote for question 5. If you were going to teach someone the lean-forward method or make a poster about this method, would it be better to present the material this way or in paragraph form? Tell why or why not.

_____

_____

_____

7. What steps did Dr. Haefeli take when he did his research? _____

_____

Why do you think the author put this paragraph before the paragraph in which he told you what the lean-forward technique was?

_____

_____

Learn More   Do your own research! Take a survey. How many people in your class have swallowed a pill before? How many people had trouble? How many would prefer a liquid to a pill if given a choice? How many would change their answer to the last question if the liquid tasted like liver? Make a bar graph that shows your results.

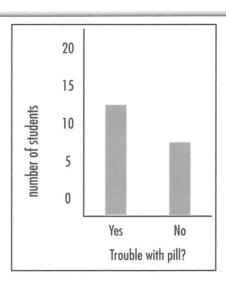

Mystery of the Water

1 "Get in here right now!" All of the children — Eloise, Jon, and Henry — came scrambling. Anxiously, they stood in front of their mother. They could tell from her voice that something was very wrong.

2 "Look at that!" The children turned and looked in the direction of their mother's extended finger. She was pointing at a trail of water on the floor. "If I've told you once, I've told you a thousand times," she said angrily, "that if you spill water, it has to be wiped up. You know that water left on the floor will discolor the wood and warp the floorboards! I can't afford to replace stained or twisted floorboards! Who did this?"

3 "Not I," Eloise said. "Wasn't me," said Jon. Henry, the youngest, said, "It was Miles."

4 Eloise and Jon hooted with laughter. Eloise said, "Henry, we know you did it. There is no way Miles could have spilled the water!"

5 "It was Miles," Henry insisted. "Miles likes to jump into the bathtub and take a bath when the water is just a few inches high. The water is from him."

6 "Cats hate water," Eloise said. "Everyone knows that," Jon said. "Not all cats hate water," Henry insisted. "There are some kinds that like it."
An expression of disbelief crossed their mother's face. "This better not happen again," she said, her voice tight.

7 Much to everyone's dismay, it happened twice more that week. Despite Eloise, Jon, and Henry insisting that it wasn't them, their mother said, "The next time I find water, every one of you will be assigned extra work."

8 That night, the children's mother started to fill the bathtub. When the water was a few inches high, Miles jumped in! When he was completely drenched, he hopped out, leaving a trail of puddles on the floor. The children's mother said, "Seeing is believing!"

Your Name: _____   Partner: _____

Mystery of the Water *(cont.)*

First   Silently read "Mystery of the Water." You might see words you do not know. There might be parts you do not understand. Keep reading! Find out what the story is mainly about.

Then   Sum up the story. Write the main actions and most important information. If someone reads your summary, that person should know it is this story you are writing about.

_____

_____

_____

_____

_____

_____

After That   Read the story again. Use a pencil to circle or mark words you don't know. Note places that confuse you. Underline the main action or idea of each paragraph.

Next   Meet with your partner. Help each other find these words in the text and decide what they mean. Tell which key words or phrases from the story help you and your partner decide.

Word	Meaning	Key Words or Phrases
discolor		
disbelief		

Think about what you figured out about the prefix *dis-*. Use your knowledge to write a short definition for the following words:

dislike _____

disagree _____

dishonest _____

disappear _____

disown _____

disconnect _____

Your Name: _____

Mystery of the Water *(cont.)*

Now   Answer the story questions below.

1. Why did the children's mother tell them she was going to assign them *all* extra work?

_____

_____

2. How do you know the children's mother finally believed Henry? In your answer, use a quote from the story.

_____

_____

_____

_____

3. In the first paragraph, you are told that, "All the children came scrambling." Describe in your own words how they came.

_____

_____

_____

Why do you think the author chose to use this word? What does this tell you about the family in the story?

_____

_____

_____

4. No one believed Henry, but he insisted it was Miles. Why do you think Henry kept insisting it was Miles? What can you infer (guess) must have happened earlier to make Henry so sure?

_____

_____

_____

_____

Your Name: _____

Mystery of the Water *(cont.)*

Then   Reread the entire story one last time. Pay attention to what Eloise and Jon said to Henry.

5. When did you find out that Miles was a cat? Were you surprised?

_____

_____

Why would some people be surprised when they found out Miles was a cat?

_____

_____

6. When Henry said that it was Miles who left the water on the floor, it says in the passage that Eloise and Jon "hooted with laughter." Why didn't the author say "Eloise and Jon laughed merrily" instead?

_____

_____

_____

7. Do you think Eloise and Jon should tell Henry they are sorry for what they said to him? Explain your answer.

_____

_____

_____

8. Now that you have read the story, how should the family fix the problem of the water on the floor? Explain.

_____

_____

_____

Learn More   Domestic cats (those who are pets) have a reputation for disliking water. However, that is not true for some cats. Do research to find the reasons why some cats dislike water and other cats like it. Create a chart that lists many reasons for each category.

Amazon Stray

 The team was more than tired. They were exhausted. They were wet, muddy, and hungry, too. They opened a can of tinned meat, and that's when Mikael, one of the team members, spotted a stray dog. The dog was looking right at him. It looked miserable. Feeling sorry for the scruffy creature, Mikael tossed the starving dog a meatball. It was a small gesture, but to the dog, it sealed the deal. He was now part of the team.

 The four human members of the team didn't yet know their team had grown to five. They were only thinking about the race they were in. The race was a grueling 430 miles. It was part of the Adventure Racing World Championship. It involved trekking, mountain biking, and kayaking. It also included navigation. Athletes had to figure out where they were and how to navigate through wild and unmarked areas. Part of what made the race so grueling was that it was non-stop. The location was a secret until the start. It took most teams 10 days to finish — if they could.

 The human team members finished their meat. Then they started on the next segment of the race. For this section, they had to trek 20 miles. The hike would be especially difficult because it was through a wet and muddy rainforest. To their surprise, the dog followed them. The dog didn't even turn back when they were in knee-deep mud!

 During the kayaking segment, the dog jumped into the water! He started swimming after them, and he would not turn back. It was heartbreaking. Finally, Mikael could stand it no longer. He stopped paddling and put the dog in his kayak. When the team crossed the finish line, the mud-splattered dog was right behind them. The dog may have been bleeding and exhausted, but he was no longer a stray. His name was Arthur, and he had a home.

Your Name: _____ Partner: _____

Amazon Stray (cont.)

First Silently read "Amazon Stray." You might see words you do not know or read parts you do not understand. Keep reading! Try to find out what the story is mainly about.

Then Sum up the story. Write the main actions and most important information. If someone reads your summary, that person should know it is this story you are writing about.

_____

_____

_____

_____

_____

After That Read the story again. Use a pencil to circle or mark words you don't know. Note places that confuse you. Underline the main action or idea of each paragraph.

Next Meet with your partner. Help each other find these words in the text.

   exhausted   grueling   trekking   navigation   segment

Read the sentences around the words. Think about how they fit in the whole story. Define the words. Write down key words or phrases from the text that help you and your partner define them. The first one is done for you.

Word	Definition	Key Words or Phrases
exhausted	really tired	The team was more than tired.
grueling		
trekking		
navigation		
segment		

Your Name: _____

Amazon Stray *(cont.)*

Now   Answer the story questions below.

1. The race had four parts. Name each part. Explain what each part is. Draw a picture.

Name of Part	What It Is	What It Looks Like

2. Why was the team surprised that the dog followed them?

_____

_____

3. What made the race grueling? Make sure you provide several reasons.

_____

_____

_____

4. There is a saying that goes, "A little kindness goes a long way." Does this story match the saying? Tell why or why not. Provide an example from the story that supports your answer.

_____

_____

_____

_____

Your Name: _____

Amazon Stray (cont.)

Then Reread the entire story one last time. Pay attention as to how paragraph 2 differs from the other paragraphs.

5. In one sentence, name the main idea of paragraph 2. _____

_____

6. Why do you think the author included the information in paragraph 2? _____

_____

_____

How does knowing these details affect how you feel when you read about the dog's actions later in the story?

_____

_____

_____

7. What can you infer from the ending of the story? What guesses can you make about what happened to the dog after the race? List at least three guesses.

_____

_____

_____

_____

Learn More Use the Internet to find out more information about Arthur. Find at least one piece of information that is not included in the story. Use what you learn to write two tweets about Arthur. (**Note:** A tweet can be no longer than 140 characters)

Key Search Terms	
◆ Arthur	◆ Sweden
◆ dog	◆ Amazon

Tweet #1: _____

_____

Tweet #2: _____

_____

Travel Danger

 "If I could travel to any planet," Renny told the class, "I would go to Venus. Venus is the second planet from the Sun. There is something very unique about it. It doesn't have any moons or rings, but that is not what makes it different."

 Renny took a deep breath before continuing his oral report. He had worked hard on his report. He had practiced saying it aloud many times at home. "What makes Venus unique is that it is the only planet that spins backward. This is why I would like to go there. The Sun doesn't rise in the east and set in the west on Venus. The sun rises in the west! It sets in the east! I would like to see that!"

 Renny continued, "Additionally, Venus rotates sluggishly. It goes so slowly that one day on Venus is longer than a year! It takes 243 Earth days for Venus to go around on its axis, but it only takes about 230 Earth days to orbit around the Sun! Can you imagine living where a day is longer than a year?" The class found it hilarious that a day could be longer than a year. The thought made them burst out laughing.

 Renny waited until everyone calmed down. "To get to Venus's surface," he said, "one has to pass through three things. One has to pass through clouds of sulfuric acid, hurricane-force winds, and lightning. The surface, when you get there, will be hot. It will be over 900 degrees Fahrenheit! This makes Venus the hottest planet in the solar system. The air on Venus is thick and poisonous. It's mostly made of carbon dioxide. If a person from Earth tried to walk on Venus, he would be crushed. The weight of the air would flatten him!"

 "One day I'll go to Venus," Renny said. "I'll go there, but I'll never travel to Earth. Most of Earth is covered in water. The water isn't frozen! It's liquid!" Renny shook his head, "Earth is just too dangerous."

Your Name: _____ Partner: _____

Travel Danger (cont.)

First Silently read "Travel Danger." You might see words you do not know. There might be parts you do not understand. Keep reading! Try to find out what the story is mainly about.

Then Sum up the entire story <u>except for the last paragraph</u>. Write the main actions and most important information. If someone reads your summary, that person should know it is this story you are writing about, not a different story!

_____

_____

_____

_____

_____

After That Read the story again. Use a pencil to circle or mark words you don't know. Note places that confuse you. Underline the main action or idea of each paragraph.

Next Meet with your partner. Help each other find these words in the text.

unique   oral   hilarious

Choose a different word than your partner from the word list above. Then be the teacher! Teach your partner what the word means. Make sure you tell your partner what part of the text helped your figure out what the word means. Write this information here:

a. My word is _____.

It means _____.

It must mean this because _____

_____

_____

Your partner will teach you about his/her chosen word. Record your partner's information.

b. My partner's word is _____.

It means _____.

He/she thinks it must mean this because _____

_____

_____

Your Name: _____

Travel Danger (cont.)

(Now)   Answer the story questions below.

1. How do you know Renny had worked hard on his report?

_____

_____

2. Where does the Sun rise and set on Venus compared to Earth?

_____

_____

What is the cause of this difference?

_____

_____

3. Renny says that Venus rotates *sluggishly*. What animal's name is in the word *sluggishly*? In the box, draw a picture of this animal. On the lines, describe how this animal moves.

_____

_____

_____

_____

Think about how the word *sluggishly* was used in the story. How does it fit with the animal?

_____

_____

_____

4. Use evidence from the story to tell why it would or would not be safe for you to visit Venus.

_____

_____

_____

_____

Your Name: _____

Travel Danger *(cont.)*

Then   Reread the entire story one last time. Pay attention to what you find out in the last paragraph.

5. Tell what you find out in the last paragraph about Renny. _____

_____

6. Why do you think the author waited until the last paragraph to let you find out? What might be the author's purpose for doing this?

_____

_____

Do you think not knowing about Renny until the end made the story better? Tell why or why not. (There is no wrong answer! It is what *you* think!)

_____

_____

7. Reread the first sentence of paragraph 3. Note how Renny uses the word *additionally*. Think of two facts about Earth. Put the facts into two sentences. Start the second sentence with the word *additionally*. Make sure you remember to put a comma after this word.

_____

_____

_____

_____

Learn More   Use the Internet or a book on planets to find out how long days and years are on other planets. Try to find out if there is liquid water on any other planet, too! Create a chart like the one below.

Planet Name	Day Length	Year Length	Liquid Water?

The Disgruntled Dentist

 "I've already scolded him, but I need you to reprimand him, too," Castor's mother told the dentist. "I've told him over and over to take care of his teeth, but he doesn't pay any attention to me. He just ignores me."

 The dentist looked at Castor's teeth. They were bright orange. "Hmmm," said the dentist. "I better take a closer look." The dentist asked Castor to hold his mouth open wide. The dentist carefully examined Castor's teeth. "I'm a bit disgruntled with you," the dentist told Castor after he finished his examination. "You deserve to be scolded. You haven't been taking care of your teeth properly. This bothers me. You know that it is very important for you to take care of your teeth."

 "I'm most concerned with your incisors," the dentist said. "You know that your incisors are the ones at the front of your mouth. You know that they are used for cutting or shearing food into small, chewable pieces. Yours are bright orange, but I can tell that you are not taking care of them. They've gotten dull. They should be sharper. You must not be eating properly. If you were eating properly, your teeth would be in better shape. They would be the right length, and they would be sharp."

 "That's what I keep telling him!" Castor's mother said. "He's got to eat better! If he doesn't, he will never be able to have a house!"
"But my teeth are orange!" Castor protested.

 The dentist spoke sternly. "Yes, the color is perfect, but I'm concerned about the length. If you don't start eating right, you won't wear down your teeth. They will get too long. You know your incisors never stop growing!"

 Castor hung his head. "Okay," he said. "I promise to eat more trees."
"Good!" Castor's mother said! "And then, like any good beaver, you can use the parts of the trees you don't eat to make a dam and lodge to live in."

Your Name: _____   Partner: _____

The Disgruntled Dentist (cont.)

For this activity, work in groups of four. If your group has fewer than four members, share the Mr./Ms. Future task. Begin by deciding who will perform each task.

Title	Student's Name	What Is Your Task?
Mr./Ms. Meaning		Explain the meanings of unfamiliar words.
Mr./Ms. Plot		Summarize what is happening in the passage.
Mr./Ms. Ask		Ask important questions about the passage.
Mr./Ms. Future		Guess what will happen next in the passage.

First   Read paragraphs 1–2 of "The Disgruntled Dentist." Then stop and perform these tasks:

Mr./Ms. Meaning: Define of the words *reprimand* and *disgruntled*. Share this information.

Mr./Ms. Plot: Summarize the events of paragraphs 1 and 2 aloud to your group. Show how knowing the words *reprimand* and *disgruntled* helps determine what is happening.

Mr./Ms. Ask: Ask one question about the characters in the passage to determine if your group members have an understanding of the passage so far.

Mr./Ms. Future: Predict what is most wrong with the son's teeth. Predict what the dentist is most disgruntled about. Use evidence from the passage.

Next   Read paragraphs 1–4 of "The Disgruntled Dentist." Stop reading and perform these tasks:

Mr./Ms. Meaning: Determine the meaning of the words *incisors* and *dull*. Share your findings.

Mr./Ms. Plot: Remind the group of what happened in paragraphs 1 and 2. Then summarize the events of paragraphs 3 and 4 aloud to your group.

Mr./Ms. Ask: Ask one question about the way the passage is written. Your question should make your group think about the way the author is revealing information about these characters and their situation.

Mr./Ms. Future: Predict what will happen next and what we will learn about these characters.

Then   Read the entire passage. As a group, do the following:

+ Discuss the ending of the story. Share thoughts and opinions.

+ Find and share quotes from the passage that give early clues about these characters.

+ Discuss the author's purpose in writing this passage. Was the author successful in achieving that purpose? Why or why not? Share your opinions with the group.

Finally   On a separate piece of paper, write a short summary of your group's discussion.

Backwards Water

 What if one could go back in time? What if one went back to the year 1800? What if one went to Chicago? Chicago is a city in Illinois, and it is built along the shore of Lake Michigan. Lake Michigan is one of the Great Lakes. A river runs through Chicago. It is called the Chicago River. In 1800, the water from the river flowed into the lake. One could throw a stick in the water, and the stick would float. The river's current would carry the stick down the river. It would carry it all the way to the lake.

 Today, this is not the case at all. Throw a stick into the waters of the Chicago River. The stick will still float. The current will still carry it down the river. However, the stick will not go into the lake. The stick will be carried *away* from the lake! Why won't the stick go into the lake?

 In 1900, the flow of the Chicago River was reversed! The water was made to flow backwards! Today, the water still flows backwards. It still flows out of the lake! How and why did this happen?

 Lake Michigan was the source of drinking water for people in Chicago. It was important to keep the water clean. Polluted water is not safe to drink. It can make people very ill. Sewage (human waste) was flowing into the lake. It and other pollutants were making the water dirty. The polluted water had made many people ill.

 Engineers got to work. They studied the river. Then, they dug a canal. The canal connected part of the Chicago River to another river. The engineers made sure to do something. They made sure the canal was deeper than the Chicago River. Think about how water flows downhill. Gravity pulls it down. Gravity pulled river water into the canal. By using gravity, the engineers reversed the river's natural flow. They made the river flow backwards!

Your Name: _____

Backwards Water (cont.)

For this activity, work in groups of four. If your group has fewer than four members, share the Mr./Ms. Future task. Begin by deciding who will perform each task.

Title	Student's Name	What Is Your Task?
Mr./Ms. Meaning		Explain the meaning of unfamiliar words.
Mr./Ms. Plot		Summarize what is happening in the passage.
Mr./Ms. Ask		Ask important questions about the passage.
Mr./Ms. Future		Guess what will happen next in the passage.

First Read paragraphs 1 and 2 of "Backwards Water." Then stop and perform these tasks:

Mr./Ms. Meaning: Determine the meanings of the words *flowed* and *current*. Share your findings.

Mr./Ms. Plot: Summarize the events of paragraphs 1 and 2 aloud to your group. Show how an understanding of the words *flowed* and *current* helps determine what is happening in the passage.

Mr./Ms. Ask: Ask one question about a place mentioned in the passage to determine if your group members have an understanding of the passage so far.

Mr./Ms. Future: Predict where the passage will go next and what the author will tell the reader next. Use evidence from the passage to justify your predictions.

Next Read paragraphs 1–4 of "Backwards Water." Then stop reading and perform these tasks:

Mr./Ms. Meaning: Determine the meanings of the words *reversed* and *polluted*. Share findings.

Mr./Ms. Plot: Remind the group of what happened in paragraphs 1 and 2. Then summarize the events of paragraphs 3 and 4 aloud to your group.

Mr./Ms. Ask: Ask one question about the way the passage is written. Your question should make your group think about the way the author is revealing information about this place and what was done to it.

Mr./Ms. Future: Predict what the author will next tell us about the Chicago River.

Then Read the entire passage. As a group, do the following:

♦ Discuss the ending of the story. Share thoughts and opinions.

♦ Find and share quotes from the passage that give early clues about what was done to the Chicago River.

♦ Discuss the author's purpose in writing this passage. Was the author successful in achieving that purpose? Why or why not? Share your opinions with the group.

Finally On a separate piece of paper, write a short summary of your group's discussion.

"Wriggling for Bones" (pages 8–11)

Summary: A scientist asks his son to go into a cave to look at some bones. The bones are very hard to get to. The bones turn out to be old and special.

Vocabulary: jagged = "rough and sharp"; *narrow* = "thin"; *chamber* = "small room or space"; *spelunker* = "cave explorer"

1. He saw photos of them.
2. One had to squeeze through an opening that was only seven and one-half inches wide, and Dr. Berger was too big.
3. Yes, because when Matt came out, he said was, "Daddy, it's wonderful!"
4. Student drawings should feature spikes or triangles. Explanations should include words like *steep, jagged,* and *sharp.*
5. The first three paragraphs focus mainly on Matt's task, while the last two paragraphs are mostly about the bones.
6. The author wanted to get the reader caught up in what Matt had to do. Matt's task is more exciting than details about the bones.

"The Ugliest Creature" (pages 12–15)

Summary: Marcella describes three creatures she believes are ugly: the monkfish, the star-nosed mole, and the blobfish. Marcella thinks she is much better looking, especially because of her arms. At the end, you find out Marcella is an octopus!

Positive Words: fortunate, beautiful

Negative Words: ugly, disgusting, hideous, repulsive, foul, horrid, revolting

1. It grows back.
2. They thought it wouldn't taste good because of the way it looks (head too big for its body; brown, warty skin; mouth filled with razor-sharp teeth; etc.).
3. "22 appendages ring its snout," "long and fleshy," "thick, pink noodles"
4. The author says that their flesh is like a mass of Jell-O.
5. In the last paragraph, Marcella says she is a blue-ringed octopus.
6. The author wanted the reader to be surprised.
7. The author wrote about Marcella's arms with the rings on them and that they were the envy of the animal world.

"Missing!" (pages 16–19)

Summary: A tourist is believed to be lost. Lots of people look for her. She wasn't lost, she had just changed her clothes. She even looked for herself!

Drawing: The hill without trees should be circled ("barren, treeless hillsides").

Vocabulary: People must flee their homes because "hot lava streams out, and ash is spewed into the air." Most likely, if one flees, one is running away or trying to escape.

1. He had counted wrong. He thought there was one more person on the bus.
2. The word *combed* is used as a verb because it describes an action.
3. They were looking carefully.
4. Yes. Iceland has "roaring" rivers and "thundering" waterfalls. Both adjectives are loud; it takes a lot of water to make a river roar and a waterfall thunder.
5. The "2" should be circled. Paragraph 2 is filled with facts about Iceland. It isn't about the missing woman.

"The Sky Is Falling!" (pages 20–23)

Summary of paragraphs 1–5: Chicken runs to Turkey to tell him that the sky is falling. They run to tell Moose. Then they all run to Skunk, and then they all run to Squirrel to tell him the bad news.

Vocabulary: humorous— "funny"; *dismal*— "not good, dire"

1. Chicken Small, Turkey Burger, and Goose Moose told her.
2. No, they all went looking for a solution.
3. *True:* The sky on the stage is falling; *False:* The real sky isn't falling.
4. Students should choose Drawing B because its cartoonish style fits the tone and content of the story better. Drawing A is too realistically drawn for the story.
5. You find out that the sky is scenery for a stage show. Pearl Squirrel doesn't get upset like the other animals. His solution is to paint a new sky and staple it.
6. Pearl Squirrel's "eyes twinkled, and his mouth began to curl up at the corners." This helps you know that Pearl Squirrel is cheerful, happy, and about to smile.
7. The "7" should be circled.

"Stay Away from My Toys!" (pages 24–27)

Summary: Robert Louis Stevenson is a famous children's author who wrote poems and also a book called *Treasure Island.* He knew how hard it was to share his toys.

Vocabulary: meddle = "to mess with, to touch or handle without permission"

1. *Facts:* born in Scotland in 1850 (2), missed a lot of school due to illness (2), had trouble fitting in (2), other children thought that he looked strange (2).
2. The author says that the book has a "one-legged seaman with a parrot on his shoulder. It also has pirates and a treasure map marked with an X."
4. adulthood; Stevenson writes about when he is "grown to man's estate."
5. The author says we are told it is good to share but it is hard to do so.
6. No, it was only about sharing; yes, it goes back to the topic of sharing.
7. *rhyming words:* estate, great; boys, toys

"Purr for the Perfect Pet" (pages 28–31)

Summary: Brian wants a pet and asks his father for specific ones. His father refuses every time and gives reasons. They agree on a cat they read about in a notice.

Vocabulary: yearned = "wanted, longed for"; *detest* = "hate"; *available* = "able to be obtained or picked up"; *dumbfounded* = "astonished, too shocked to speak"

1. He couldn't pet a fish, and it couldn't sit on his lap.
2. *first:* dog; *second:* hamster; *third:* canary
3. He liked the way they chirped. "Birds should not be kept in cages," or, "They should be allowed to soar through the air."
5. chipmunk, squirrel
6. Brian goes to get a cat, but it is not a house cat. It is a cheetah!
7. Students will most likely say they thought of a house cat, because house pets are usually small, domestic animals. The author most likely wants readers to be surprised, because they were not expecting someone to have a cheetah for a house pet and they might not have known that cheetahs make a chirping sound.

"Boom!" (pages 32–35)

Summary: In 1916, an explosion happens in a tunnel, filling it with smoke and gas. A man named Garrett Morgan used a new invention called a safety hood to save lives.

Vocabulary: vented = "flowed, entered into"; *ignited* = "lit or started"; *pleaded* = "begged or asked"; *emerged* = "came out or into view"

1. Gas came in from under the lake bed and ignited, causing an explosion.
2. Smoke rises; tubes near the ground bring up the cleaner air below the smoke.
3. He came as fast as he could. He did not waste time changing his clothes.
4. The dialogue should show that both understand the urgency of the situation.
7. They trusted the hoods after they saw them being used by Morgan.

"The Right Feet" (pages 36–39)

Summary: Three characters are talking about how badly one character's feet hurt. It turns out she has put her shoes on the wrong feet. She refuses to believe this.

1. She was feeling a terrible pain in her feet.

2. She didn't know there were left-footed shoes and right-footed shoes.

3. *Possible answers:* sharp, stinging, mean, annoyed

4. Accept appropriate responses that show the personalities of the characters.

5. a. Patti's feet hurt; b. Her shoes should be put on the correct feet; c. No, because she doesn't believe her friends; d. We are given enough information to fix it when Hugo speaks for the last time at the end of the play.

6. Patti wonders if she broke a bone; Julie says that she has broken one before.

"A Finger Where?" (pages 40–43)

Summary: This story is about capuchin monkeys. Two games the monkeys play are described, as well as how they learn how to eat palm nuts.

Vocabulary: exchange = "trade or pass back and forth"; *facial* = "of or on the face"; *gregarious* = "social"; *discarded* = "thrown away"

1. It swings back and forth while keeping its finger up the other's nose.

2. 12 to 22 inches long; We are told that the tails are as long as the bodies, and the bodies are 12 to 22 inches long.

3. swim with friends; Capuchin monkeys are gregarious, and that is why they are social and like to do things together.

4. The adults pick up the fruit; they bring it to a place with stones; they smash it open with the stones; they eat the nut inside.

5. Paragraph 1 is about a game with fingers in noses. Paragraph 2 is about a game where one bites off facial hair.

6. to make you interested or puzzled; it is a hint because females don't generally have facial hair, and people don't bite hair off of each other's faces.

"When Morning Is Afternoon" (pages 44–47)

Summary: Four people have a meeting at the same time. The people live in different time zones, so the time of day is different for each of them.

1. Students should draw hands on clocks to illustrate the following times: Aya, 8:00 p.m.; Ben, 2:00 p.m.; Lizzy, 11:00 a.m.; Yuki, 3:00 a.m.

2. Yuki; Japan's time is 13 hours ahead of the time in Washington, DC.

3. Accept appropriate responses. In their own words, students should state that time zones help us know where it is morning on Earth and where it is night.

4. Answers may vary for the first part of the question. For the second part, students should say that Yuki is the least likely person to have scheduled the meeting. He says the time is "not convenient" and he will be "exhausted."

5. that everyone was at the same meeting

6. The author wanted the reader to feel surprised or to wonder how it was possible.

"Life-Saving Haircut" (pages 48–51)

Summary: A sheep named Chris needed a haircut. The haircut saved his life because Chris's wool was half his weight, which made it difficult for him to see or move. Chris missed his annual haircut because he had wandered off into the Australian bush.

Vocabulary: aid = "help or rescue"; *mammoth* = "extremely large"; *annual* = "once a year"; *hooves* = "type of animal feet"; *nimble* = "able to move easily"

1. He missed his annual haircuts because he wandered off.

2. "Chris looked like nothing but a mammoth ball of filthy wool."

3. It was cut in half. You would weigh 100 pounds. In the story, it says, "His weight had been cut in half!" Half of 200 pounds is 100 pounds.

4. When you shear something, you cut it. So when *shear* is a verb, it means "to cut." *Shears* as a noun is the thing you cut with.

5. Just like Chris, they might have a hard time seeing, the extra weight could damage their hooves, and they might have a hard time walking.

6. You are told about things you might think of when it comes to helping someone. You are told Chris was saved by a haircut.

7. to make you want to keep reading to find out how a haircut could save a life

"Riddles and More Riddles" (pages 52–55)

Summary: The story is about a teacher named Ms. Boggle who asks her students three riddles. The students ask Ms. Boggle a riddle, too.

Vocabulary: Synonyms = *perplexed* and *baffled.* Both mean "puzzled, confused." The other word is *glee.* Possible synonyms for this word: *joy, happiness,* etc.

1. He or she might say, "I'm having trouble learning how to do this." Or, he or she might say, "I need some help so I can understand this better."

3. No, because a mile is way too long; the author wanted you to know that Ms. Boggle felt really happy.

4. clap her hands in glee; that is what she did when she thought of the answer for the egg riddle.

5. The first paragraph is not about riddles. It is about attitude.

"The Amazing World of Ants" (pages 56–59)

Summary: Ants are amazing. The driver ant is used to sew up cuts. The leafcutter ant grows fungus in its garden. The bulldog ant is fierce and will attack itself.

Vocabulary: remote = "far away, by itself"; *inhospitable* = "unfriendly, unwelcoming"

1. When someone uses it to sew up a gash or cut.

2. They go out with other ants; you are told they go in a convoy (a group) because they can protect each other.

3. the bulldog ant; people don't want to get stung.

4. *Both:* have to fertilize it, weed it; *People Gardens:* grow many things, grow in ground or pots; *Ant Gardens:* grow fungus, grow in a huge pile

"Nothing New to Invent" (pages 60–63)

Summary: Rose needs to invent something, but she thinks everything has already been invented. When her friends invent something, she invents a story about it.

Vocabulary: words about irritation: *peevish, exasperated,* and *frustration;* word about wishing for something: *wistfully*

1. She thought everything had already been invented.

2. ocean-sofa and dino-rider

3. Rose got an idea; a real lightbulb did not turn on.

4. fiction; there are no ocean-sofas, dino-riders, or cloaks of invisibility.

5. Rose needs to invent something new. Her solution is to invent a story.

6. The author wants to keep you wondering about what Rose can invent.

"Insult or Compliment?" (pages 64–67)

Summary: Some people think being called a birdbrain is an insult, but the author says some birds can be smart. Crows are birds that can solve analogy puzzles.

1. The author wasn't insulted. She took it as a compliment.
2. They might think they are being called stupid. They may think birds aren't smart because they have small brains.
3. *Puzzles* is a plural noun. It is naming things. *Puzzle* is a verb. It is describing the action of solving something or figuring it out.
4. The answer is "HI," because the crow will have learned that double letters go together. "FG" and "HI" are not double letters, whereas "HH" and "II" are.
5. Paragraph 2 explains what an analogy is and provides examples; no, because there is nothing in paragraph 2 about birds or being insulted. It is only about analogies.
6. It's written in first person. The character says things like, "I know I am smart."
7. No. the author thinks getting upset over insults is a waste of brain power.

"Mouse Feelings" (pages 68–71)

Summary: Cesar sees a mouse and tells how he hates them but loves dogs. Next, Cesar listens to a story about a dog that fell off a boat. The dog swam to an island and was able to survive for five weeks because there were mice to eat.

Vocabulary: presumed = "thought to be or believed"; *loathe* = "hate, strongly dislike"; *detest* = "hate, strongly dislike"

Possible opposites: like, admire, love

1. Dakota showed them a video on his phone.
2. She swam to the island and then caught mice to eat.
3. Drawing A. She was "skinny and a bit malnourished."
4. Yes. Accept appropriate responses.
5.
6. Cesar and his dislike of mice; Tuna and how she survived
7. No. Accept appropriate responses.
8. Paragraphs 5, 6, and 8 should be circled. Accept appropriate responses.

"Down It Goes!" (pages 72–75)

Summary: The story tells how pills are important when you are sick, but that they may be hard to swallow. You are given a doctor's technique for swallowing pills.

Vocabulary: prescription = "note from the doctor for pills"; *loathe* = "hate"; *traumatic* = "upsetting"; *technique* = "way of doing something"

1. They have trouble swallowing them.
2. They said they would pay a dime for every pill swallowed. Answers to second part of question will vary.
3. Answers will vary. Students may say that the lean-forward technique is better because research shows that it works for a lot of people.
4. Yes, because the author writes that there is a problem because the medicine doesn't taste like bubble gum or green apples. That's only a problem if everyone likes the flavors.
5. Step 1: Put the pill on your tongue; Step 2: Take a medium sip of water; Step 3: Lean your head forward as you swallow.
6. Answers may vary. Students may say it is better to put it as written in question 5 because it is easier to follow.
7. He asked questions and did tests on 150 people. Readers will be more likely to think that the technique will work.

"Mystery of the Water" (pages 76–79)

Summary: Three children — Eloise, Jon, and Henry — are blamed for water on the floor. No one believes Henry when he says that the cat did it. The mother finally believes it only when she sees the cat jump into the bathtub.

Vocabulary: discolor = "ruin the color of, stain"; *disbelief* = "not believing it is real"; *dislike* = "to not like something"; *disagree* = "to not agree"; *dishonest* = "not honest"; *disappear* = "to not appear"; *disown* = "to not own anymore"; *disconnect* = "to not connect anymore"

1. She thought one of them was leaving the water but didn't know which one.
2. When she saw Miles jump in the bathtub water, she said, "Seeing is believing."
3. Accept appropriate responses that show the urgency with which the children responded to their mother's call.
4. He must have seen Miles get into the bathtub before.
5. You find out in paragraph 6 when Eloise tells Henry that all cats hate water. Many people think that cats hate water.
6. When one hoots with laugher, one is making fun of someone. When one laughs merrily, one is laughing because they are having a good time. Eloise and Jon were making fun of Henry.

"Amazon Stray" (pages 80–83)

Summary: A stray dog joins a team of four people when one of them tosses it a meatball. The team is competing in a 430-mile race through the jungle. The dog never leaves them, even when they have to go through mud and water.

Vocabulary: grueling = "really hard"; *trekking* = "hiking"; *navigation* = "finding out where you are and where to go"; *segment* = "part of something"

1. trekking (hiking); mountain biking (using a bicycle); kayaking (paddling on water); navigation (finding one's way)
2. They went through knee-deep mud and also through water in a kayak.
3. It was non-stop; went for 430 miles; and took place in a wet, muddy rainforest.
4. Yes. It may have been a small gesture to Mikael to toss the meatball to the dog, but it was enough to make the dog follow the team, even when it was very hard.
5. The main idea is that the race is very difficult and grueling.
6. Answers will vary. If you didn't know how hard the race is, you wouldn't know how hard it was for the dog to follow them. Knowing this may make you admire the dog more because you know what he went through.

"Travel Danger" (pages 84–87)

Summary: Renny gives an oral report about the planet Venus. He shares facts about the temperature, the air, how it spins, and the length of a day and a year.

Vocabulary: unique = "stands out, is different, one of a kind" (Venus is different; it's the only planet that spins backward.); *oral* = "spoken" (Renny is giving an oral report, which he is saying aloud.); *hilarious* = "really funny" (The kids start laughing.)

1. The story tells us that he had practiced saying it aloud many times.
2. On Earth, the Sun rises in the east and sets in the west. On Venus, it is the opposite. The cause of this difference is that Venus spins in the opposite direction that Earth spins.
3. The word *sluggishly* contains the word *slug*. A slug moves very slowly. This fact fits with the story because, just like a slug, Venus moves very slowly.
4. Answers will vary, but accept anything about heat or atmosphere.
5. Renny isn't from Earth, and he thinks liquid water is dangerous.

The lessons and activities included in *Close Reading with Text-Dependent Questions* meet the following Common Core State Standards for grade 3. (©Copyright 2010. National Governors Association Center for Best Practices and Council of Chief State School Officers. All rights reserved.)

The code for each standard covered in this resource is listed in the table below and on page 96. The codes are listed in boldface, and the unit numbers of the activities that meet that standard are listed in regular type. For more information about the Common Core State Standards and for a full listing of the descriptions associated with each code, go to *http://www.corestandards.org/* or visit *http://www.teachercreated.com/standards/*.

Here is an example of an English Language Arts (ELA) code and how to read it:

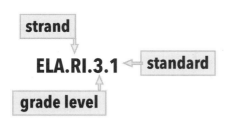

ELA Strands
L = Language
W = Writing
RI = Reading: Informational Text
RL = Reading: Literature
RF = Reading: Foundational Skills
SL = Speaking and Listening

+ +

Strand Reading: Informational Text   **Substrand** Key Ideas and Details
ELA.RI.3.1: Units 1–22
ELA.RI.3.2: Units 1–22
ELA.RI.3.3: Units 1, 3, 7, 9–10, 13, 15, 17, 19

Strand Reading: Informational Text   **Substrand** Craft and Structure
ELA.RI.3.4: Units 1–22
ELA.RI.3.5: Units 1–22
ELA.RI.3.6: Units 1–10, 12–15, 17–22

Strand Reading: Informational Text   **Substrand** Integration of Knowledge and Ideas
ELA.RI.3.7: Units 3–4, 15–16
ELA.RI.3.8: Units 1–22

Strand Reading: Informational Text   **Substrand** Range of Reading and Level of Text Complexity
ELA.RI.3.10: Units 1–22

+ +

Strand Language   **Substrand** Conventions of Standard English
ELA.L.3.1: Units 1–22
ELA.L.3.2: Units 1–22

Strand Language   **Substrand** Knowledge of Language
ELA.L.3.3: Units 1–22

Strand Language   **Substrand** Vocabulary Acquisition and Use
ELA.L.3.4: Units 1–22
ELA.L.3.5: Units 1–22
ELA.L.3.6: Units 1–22

Strand Reading: Foundational Skills **Substrand** Phonics and Word Recognition
ELA.RF.3.3: Units 1–22

Strand Reading: Foundational Skills **Substrand** Fluency
ELA.RF.3.4: Units 1–22

Strand Reading: Literature **Substrand** Range of Reading and Level of Text Complexity
ELA.RL.3.10: Units 2, 4–6, 8, 10, 12, 14, 16, 18, 20–21

Strand Reading: Literature **Substrand** Key Ideas and Details
ELA.RL.3.1: Units 2, 4–6, 8, 10, 12, 14, 16, 18, 20–21
ELA.RL.3.2: Units 2, 4–6, 8, 10, 12, 14, 16, 18, 20–21
ELA.RL.3.3: Units 2, 4, 6, 8, 10, 12, 14, 16, 18, 20–21

Strand Reading: Literature **Substrand** Craft and Structure
ELA.RL.3.4: Units 2, 4–6, 8, 10, 12, 14, 16, 18, 20–21
ELA.RL.3.5: Units 2, 4–6, 8, 10, 12, 14, 16, 18, 20–21
ELA.RL.3.6: Units 2, 4–6, 8, 10, 14, 18, 20–21

Strand Speaking and Listening **Substrand** Comprehension and Collaboration
ELA.SL.3.1: Units 1–22
ELA.SL.3.3: Units 3, 5–6, 20–22

Strand Speaking and Listening **Substrand** Presentation of Knowledge and Ideas
ELA.SL.3.4: Units 3, 5–6, 20–22
ELA.SL.3.6: Units 20–22

Strand Writing **Substrand** Text Types and Purposes
ELA.W.3.1: Units 1–20
ELA.W.3.2: Units 1–20
ELA.W.3.3: Units 2, 5–11, 13, 17, 19

Strand Writing **Substrand** Production and Distribution of Writing
ELA.W.3.4: Units 1, 4, 6, 9, 11, 13–15, 17–20

Strand Writing **Substrand** Research to Build and Present Knowledge
ELA.W.3.7: Units 1–22
ELA.W.3.8: Units 1–22

Strand Writing **Substrand** Range of Writing
ELA.W.3.10: Units 1–22
